DESPERAT

CHRONICLES OF A DESPERATE DAD

Mark Richards was for many years a dull person with a suit, a mortgage, a wife and slightly more than 2.4 children. One morning he woke up with a mid life crisis and began performing stand up comedy and writing a weekly column about his family. Despite now taking several tablets each day the condition persists.

You've probably realised by now that I'm not much of a new man. In addition to failing with the Yorkshires, you may as well know that while Jane's been away I have not done any cleaning. Nor have I washed any clothes, done any ironing, been shopping (except for beer, sweets and Yorkshire Puddings), changed the beds or got anything ready for school tomorrow.

The bit I hated most was putting my hand into the slime to get their toys – the bridge and the diver and all the other junk we imagine makes a goldfish happy. One day I felt something new down there. I sighed, stuck my hand in again and pulled out Lara Croft.

I was sitting peacefully at my desk when Jane phoned. "Have you got Tom's shoe?" she demanded.

"What? I'm at work…"

"Well you're no damn use are you?" she said, and slammed the phone down.

"So when could you do my vasectomy?" I asked, hopefully staring at the 'next year's appointments' section of my diary.

"Next Thursday," she said. "Two o'clock or three thirty."

I gulped. "That's rather sudden."

"We get a lot of cancellations," she said. "Some men get cold feet."

It wasn't my feet I was worrying about.

"Don't leave your jeans on the bedroom floor," my Dad once told me. When I asked why he said, "Well, if there's a fire in the night, you might trip over your jeans and not be able to escape." Even Dad must have known that was ridiculous. I couldn't sleep for trying to work out the odds on such an unlikely double. The trouble is, I'm now capable of exactly the same stupidity.

I spent most of Christmas morning under the dining room table. This had nothing to do with the Christmas Eve celebrations and everything to do with Frodo Baggins.

Worse followed on Boxing Day when Granny arrived with a shoot-em-up. Swiftly cast in the role of James Bond's assistant, I walked straight into the swimming pool and drowned myself.

Far below me my daughter has just crashed off her sledge and somersaulted ten yards down the slope. Hopefully she's OK. I am too cold to have any stronger feelings.

Not that Jane didn't give me instructions before she went away for the weekend. The list was pinned to the fridge. It was quite detailed – well, it ran to three pages if you want the truth. We sent twenty thousand troops to Iraq with less information.

"So where do you want to go on holiday?"

The answer – if Tom and Jessica were left to make the decision – would be Carphone Warehouse. Right now a week spent looking at mobile phones seems to be their idea of Heaven. Somewhere hot with a pool and a vat of cold beer is so far down the list it's out of sight.

I can see some major clashes looming on the music front. I took Tom and Jessica shopping for new trainers at the weekend. Somehow we ended up in HMV – an increasingly powerful magnet. "Look at this," I said cheerfully, "All the ones that I like are only five quid."

"Right, Dad," said Little Miss Sarcastic. "That's because they're all dead."

My thoughts drifted back to the homework Tom had been doing at the weekend. It was a project on the Second World War – all about smiling children being evacuated and resolute fathers building Anderson shelters.

"It's a good job there isn't a war on now isn't it, Dad?" he'd said. "Our family would be dead in ten minutes if you had to build the shelter."

Heaven help me, the wretched woman I'm married to has decided we're going to build a patio. I'm the man who broke his toe tripping over some flat pack furniture – now I'm supposed to be auditioning for Ground Force.

I was talking to a childless friend of mine the other day – or rather he was talking and I was having a visit from the green-eyed monster. "It was our anniversary last week," he said. "We went to Florence."

"Lovely," I said, through gritted teeth. It was our anniversary the other week as well. We went to Tesco.

Two days on I vaguely remember that Tom sold it to us on the grounds of 'teamwork' – as though the Xbox is the modern equivalent of the Boy Scouts. And there was something about 'making friends in different countries,' as well. Given that the only sounds we've heard since it arrived are 'Good kill,' 'Cover me,' and 'Waste the sniper,' global harmony seems a little way off at the moment.

A security man was wearing an 'I've nailed Al-Qaeda' expression. Jane was looking furious and Ben was howling. "I'm sorry, Madam," I heard him say. "We have to confiscate all potentially lethal weapons." He was triumphantly waving Ben's plastic gun – another victory in the war on terror. So much for my bacon and eggs – it looked like I'd be posting bail.

So while the family slapped on the factor ten, I scoured Greece in the Citroen Jumpy. I pulled up outside a likely looking taverna. An old woman in traditional black sat on the front step, a 12 bore shotgun resting on her knees. Either migrating sparrows were in season or you cancelled a booking at your peril.

Every year – in true festive spirit – I force my children to go carol singing. Or I did until this year. Tom claimed an urgent appointment with the Xbox, and Jessica refused to desert Colin Jackson on *Strictly Come Dancing*. Or maybe they've just become too cool to be seen carol singing with their Dad.

Chronicles of a

DESPERATE DAD

Mark Richards

ISBN–13: 978 0 9553637-0-2
ISBN–10: 0 9553637-0-5

A CIP catalogue record for this book is available from the British Library.

Cover design by Blackdogsquare Studios
(www.blackdogsquare-design.co.uk)

Cover caricature by Martin Pope
(www.martinpope.co.uk)

Prepared and printed by:
York Publishing Services Ltd
64 Hallfield Road
Layerthorpe
York YO31 7ZQ

Website: www.yps-publishing.co.uk

Publisher:
Desperate Dad Books
57/58 The Sitwell Centre
Scarborough
YO12 5EX

www.desperatedad.co.uk
01723 500366

To my children

In the hope that one day when you're a desperate parent and I'm just a photo on the mantelpiece you'll re-read these columns and say, "Yes, that was my Dad. Moderately insane, but he loved us…"

The great majority of these columns were originally published in the *Hartlepool Mail*. References to 'Pools throughout the columns are to Hartlepool United FC. The period covered by the columns was one of unremitting frustration for 'Pools who twice reached the end of season play-offs, only to snatch defeat from the jaws of victory against Bristol City and Sheffield Wednesday. At least their fans went home happy.

Contents

Acknowledgements

My first thanks must go to Paul Napier. If he hadn't said, "And we'd quite like a new columnist" one night at a Writers' Circle meeting I'd have spent many more years reading other people's columns and thinking "I could do that," instead of churning out my 600 words a week. As well as Paul, my thanks go to all the other editors and assistant editors who have followed him.

Ever since the columns started it has been a regular Monday morning routine for Sally Chandler to make herself a coffee, wish she had a cigarette and proof read the latest column. Thanks, Sal.

My thanks go to everyone at York Publishing Services for their patience in answering my never ending stream of e-mails and phone calls. And to Martin Pope, for the caricature and for giving me something else to worry about – beer cans. Sincere thanks also go to Pete at Blackdogsquare Studios – for rescuing the website, for the front cover and for telling me to stop worrying!

Little did my Dad realise when he told me not to leave my jeans on the floor in case there was a fire during the night and I fell over them trying to escape, that it would be useful copy a few decades later.

Thanks, Dad, for all you said, didn't say and imprinted on my memory. To my Mum, thank you for everything. I hope I told you in time.

And to my wife and my children. Just 'thank you' – for being there, for supporting me and for managing to do or say something each week that sparked a column. To think I once watched the children collecting conkers by a stream and prayed that one of them would fall in. "Please," I thought, "I've nothing to write about this week. It's shallow, you'll be alright…" What a dreadful father.

The Party Bag

Somewhere in hell two spits are slowly turning. On one of them, roasting for all eternity, is the man who first said "paperless office." Next to him, the flames even hotter if parents have anything to do with it, is the hapless soul who invented the Party Bag.

I was reading to Ben the other night. The door banged downstairs – Jessica back from her party. She barged into the room. "Daddy," she stormed, "George's party bag was absolutely rubbish – all it had in it was cake!" Well, that's that isn't it? George's parents will just have to spend the rest of their life in exile. A Party Bag with only cake in it – you can't sink much lower than that.

In case you've spent the last few years in a cave, a Party Bag is something your children bring home from other children's parties. No, I know we didn't have them when we were kids, but we didn't have Grandparents' Day or Halloween either. It's called progress. On the off chance that you don't want to join George's parents in exile, here's what an acceptable Party Bag contains:

- A super-bouncy ball, for bouncing in the kitchen – ideally it will go perilously close to – or with luck, actually hit – your best china

1

- Several luridly coloured gobstoppers or chewy things. These will be full of "E" numbers and are precision timed to send your children ballistic at exactly bedtime
- A lolly on a stick, covered in super-adhesive instant-bond-to-your-carpet wrapping paper
- A ridiculous game complete with minuscule silver ball that any child under two is certain to swallow
- A whistle – enough said
- And finally – and least importantly – a piece of cake

A Party Bag also comes with guarantees. It guarantees a fight. Jessica enters the house with a Party Bag – the boys fall on her demanding their share. Instantly the walls reverberate to the sound of "Not Fair!!" Blows will be traded and pretty soon we'll be reaching for something a lot stronger than Ribena.

So, spare a thought for George's parents as they leave for the colonies. Not that we can talk. We made the colossal mistake of having Tom's first ever party at home. "At home?" his friends' parents said when we gave them the invitation.

Then they sucked in their breath and shook their heads in the same way that a garage mechanic does when he gives you the estimate. "At home," they muttered again, "That's very...brave." On balance though, we escaped quite lightly. We had Tom and eight of his friends: the building society were really nice about the further advance to cover the carpet cleaning.

Of course, one day we'll look back on these halcyon days of hyper-activity and food fights and God-knows-what ground into the carpet. Ten years from now my children will all be teenagers. "Dad," Tom will languidly suggest, "Why don't you and Mum go for your hip replacements this weekend? We thought we might, er... have a few friends round. A bit of a party, you know..."

We'd certainly know what to expect. Our next door neighbours went away for the weekend recently, leaving their two teenage daughters behind. We finally fell asleep at four in the morning and woke up to a drive littered with empty pizza boxes and discarded boyfriends.

So on balance, maybe the Party Bag's not such a bad idea after all. Enjoy it while you can...

Don't Go Shopping

We went shopping the other day. Even for a man, I'm not much good at it. We're doing the lounge, which hasn't been decorated for far too long. Jane's patience has snapped and the textured wallpaper (which may well have been quite trendy around the time England won the World Cup) will have to go. So too will the settees, which I bought before we were married. Jane now tells me she has hated them for twelve years: I wasn't aware of this because she hasn't given me any subtle hints – that is, she hasn't said, "I hate these settees."

Anyway I have a day off work and we are shopping for "things" – I don't know what things but I've been told my opinion is important. Heaven knows why, as every time I say anything I receive a pitying look, plus a comment along the lines of, "Do you realise you have now suggested a red three piece, orange curtains and a yellow carpet?"

Anyway, our search for "things" leads us to Debenhams. In my opinion it's time it led us to a sandwich and a beer, but there's no chance of that. As far as furniture goes, I've got this thing about minimalism – you know the clean lines and uncluttered rooms you see in Sunday supplements. One solitary ornament standing in the middle of a

4

virginal mantelpiece – not a card, swimming certificate, coffee cup, wooden cat, M&S voucher, crayon or set of keys in sight.

So far I've spent the whole morning going on about my fantasy minimalist lounge like a broken record. I have completely forgotten that we live in a house with three children. Jane has just let it wash over her – it's the price she's prepared to pay to get me out shopping. But I have the ominous feeling that her patience is beginning to wear a little thin.

"I know," I say, suddenly becoming Mr. Useful Husband, "We need some new knives and forks – maybe we can buy them here." My wife smiles – the smile of a woman who knows her Rip van Winkle of a husband hasn't been shopping for a very long time. I duly find a set of knives and forks that I like. Jane probably doesn't like them, but it doesn't matter because she knows we're not going to buy them. How does she know this? Because I turn them over and see the price. "Fifty quid?" I shout. "Fifty quid for some knives and forks!"

"That's what they cost this year," she says. "Last time you bought some – for the Coronation – they may have been cheaper, but I'm sorry that's what they cost."

"I can't believe it – fifty quid? That's not very minimalist is it?"

Something snaps inside my wife. She turns and stares at me. She hisses at me through gritted teeth. "Will you please stop wittering about stupid bloody minimalist?"

Now the sweet, lovely girl I married is starting to shout, right in the middle of Debenhams. "Our house is never going to be minimalist." Oh God, a crowd is gathering...

"Number one, we have three children." They haven't had this much fun since bear baiting was abolished.

"Number two, it costs the earth and you are a cheapskate and..." The women in the crowd are starting to cheer.

"And number three, you'll never have minimalist because... Because you are the untidiest pig I have ever met!"

Fortunately we are in the bedding department. I look round to see which one I should crawl under. The last thing I see is my wife being carried shoulder high round Debenhams by radical feminists...

Flattened by a Flat Pack

It's now about twenty years since I stuck a chisel into my wife's hand. She was my girlfriend then, and we were building our first chair together. We still got married though – Jane's quite forgiving like that.

Over the years it is fair to say that my DIY skills have not improved. This is another cross Jane has to bear, although I did think she over-reacted slightly when the shelves I fitted on Good Friday fell down on Easter Monday. I told her straight – "It's your own fault for putting plates on them…"

But even fools like me should have been saved the advent of the Swedish furniture industry and flat packs that actually fit together. There are people – you may be one of them, if so I hate you – who can open up an Ikea package, not bother looking at the instructions and say, "Ah, yes, that goes there, that dowel over there, that locking nut needs a twist…" Thirty minutes later they present their wife with a fully functioning wardrobe.

I am not one of those people. Put quite simply, I cannot understand the instructions unless Jane is translating for me. Yes, I know the instructions are only pictures – but without my translator I simply can't relate the drawing to whatever piece it is I'm supposed to be holding.

My problems are compounded by the evil spirit who lives in the cupboard under our stairs. He takes demonic possession of me every time I go in there for my tool box. Jane has a name for him. I'd share it with you but this is a family newspaper – suffice it to say that he renders me totally incompetent and *very* bad tempered...

So nothing much has changed since the chisel incident, and over the years I have hurled abuse at innocent desks and tables, heaped scorn on the entire Swedish nation (if they can't write instructions, how can they manage our football team?) and made violent gestures at any building on a trading estate brave enough to fly a blue and yellow flag.

About four weeks ago the flat packs took their revenge. It was time to do Jessica's bedroom: she was overdue for a desk, a wardrobe, and a new bed. Hers is the smallest bedroom, so it was going to be one of those cunning arrangements where the bed's on stilts and the wardrobe and desk fit underneath. Jane and I duly went to Ikea, endured the three mile trek round it, and came out with a large number of flat packs. Carefully, and with only a minor hernia, they were carried upstairs and laid on the floor of our bedroom. Assembly would begin the next morning, and given my supreme skill in these matters, Jessica had been promised her new bedroom for Christmas 2005...

At around three in the morning, the sound of Ben crying woke me up: it was real crying, I've-just-had-a-nightmare crying. I leapt out of bed, wanting to reach him as quickly as I could, desperate to stop him waking the whole house.

Of course, I forgot about the flat pack lying on the floor. It seized it's chance and attacked me when I was half way to the door. Bang – little toe, full speed. Jane woke up to Ben screaming and me on the floor whimpering like a dog. Amazingly she ignored her injured husband and went straight to her child.

Anyway, the doctor says the break will heal quite well, but there's no point strapping it. "Just go and buy yourself some good, strong pain killers". So much for the Swedes – I can hear Sven laughing from here…

Brotherly, Sisterly Love

If you have children you'll know that they like to have a little punch-up from time to time. Christmas and Easter are always a special favourite in our house, but any time they're together will do. As I write this Tom and Jessica are happily playing on their Game Boys – an hour ago they were inflicting serious damage on each other. When she's in the right mood, Jessica can escalate hostilities faster than George Bush slipping down the poll ratings. If we hear "Get out my bedroom" at 120 decibels then it's time to batten down the hatches.

Tom's not one for direct confrontation, not initially anyway. In football terms he's more your off the ball merchant – a sly foul when he thinks the ref's not looking. Not Jessica, though – she's in-your-face, serious aggression. If she's provoked, it's a full frontal Eric Cantona, and Tom currently has the scars to prove it. And then what does she do, as she is sent packing to her bedroom? Halfway up the stairs she pauses, sticks out her chin and yells. "He deserved it!"

"Jessica, Tom did not deserve that…"

"Yes he did, he was *asking* for it!"

If you meet this girl in twenty years time, I strongly advise you not to steal her parking space.

But what do you do? It's been a hard day, you're clutching on to your beer, all you want is peace and quiet, and there are two of your children rolling on the floor tearing lumps out of each other... I don't know about you but my normal reaction is, "For God's sake you two – you are driving me insane. Any more of this and you will be in your bedrooms for a week/ never eat another sweet as long as you live/sleeping in the garage." (Choose whichever option you think is most likely to work).

Is that the correct approach? Absolutely not apparently. We have an American book, (*Siblings without Rivalry* from Piccadilly Press, if you want to read it). Next time you're not sure whether the noise from the lounge is your beloved offspring or Genghis Khan and the Mongol hordes popping round for the weekend, try this. You put down the beer, stick your head round the door and say something like, "Hi there you two, I see you're having a little disagreement. Tom, honey, why don't you share your feelings with Jessica. We *know* she'll appreciate how you feel..."

Obviously we thought we'd try that approach, so we waited all of thirty seconds for an argument to break out, then Jane (using her best *Cheers* accent) bravely went in and used those very words. Go ahead and see what happens – we haven't laughed so much since Jessica's school report suggested she was a gentle, angelic child who was a little bit quiet in class.

What did the children say to this American parenting wisdom? "I am *not* (kick) sharing anything with her!" "I don't *care* (savage thump) how he feels!"

11

Now if you'll excuse me, there's a small riot in the lounge. I'm just going to shut the door so I can't hear it, then I'm going to share my feelings with Jane – the feelings about having another beer, that is...

Half Man, Half Fish

We were at Center Parcs last week and I kept thinking about fish. The Atlantic Salmon to be precise, as featured on the BBC. It's the sort of nature programme they like so much that it's on every six months, so you may well have seen it. Why was I worrying about salmon when I should have been cheerfully cycling through Sherwood Forest? Because Tom and Jessica kept taking me down the rapids, that's why...

If you have seen it, you'll know the programme starts with the young, athletic salmon bravely leaving the safety and calm of the breeding ground and swimming powerfully out to the Atlantic. Eventually they will return home to mate and then die. But some of them don't make it. Exhausted by the journey and swimming against the tide, they can't quite get themselves up that last waterfall into the peaceful waters of the spawning ground. The brown bears know this, and they're lying in wait, licking their lips in anticipation. "Oh look Dad," the children always say when we watch it, "They're eating all the old, tired ones..."

Sadly, that's now me on the rapids – an old, tired salmon who can't quite make it over the last jump. And to think that the first time Tom ever wanted to go down I checked it first. Was he a good enough swimmer? Were the currents too strong? Were the plunge pools too deep? I'm still full of trepidation, but these days it's not for Tom.

They've taken to racing me now. A flash of her purple cossy and Jessica's off. Tom hurls himself headlong into the first bend. "Hey you two, wait for me." But it's no use – they're gone. I bump slowly along, occasionally coming to a stop as I get beached in the shallows. I can just see them at the first jump – an effortless flip and Jess is over it, Tom crashing through behind her. For a split second I'm stuck on top of the jump, but then another middle aged salmon comes along, helplessly out of control. Inevitably, one of her flailing limbs catches me in the head. We crash round a corner together. "Sorry," she grunts.

"No problem," I gasp, as my elbow collides violently with the side.

Tom and Jessica are waiting at the bottom. "We'll give you a start this time, Dad…thirty seconds." Oh great. It makes no difference of course, and they overtake me between the first and second jumps. I struggle gamely on, finally coming to the last jump. There's a rope at the side of it and with a small prayer of thanks I haul myself up and over – then I get beached again on the other side. As I desperately try to paddle forwards I can almost hear the bears cheering: "This one's not going to make it, lads. Another one for us – and it's a nice fat one…"

But then salvation arrives in the unlikely shape of my nemesis from the previous race. If anything she's even more out of control this time. She crashes into me and knocks me head first into the final plunge pool. I'm just struggling to the surface when she lands on me. "Ee, sorry, love," she says. "That were grand, weren't it? I'm off round again. What about you…"

A Death in the Family

I went mad a couple of years ago and bought some goldfish. We'd been to the Fair, and somehow it hadn't seemed quite right to be going home without one of those little plastic bags. The next day the only parking space I could find was outside Peter's Pet Shop. "Come on," I said to Tom and Jessica on impulse, "I'll treat you."

"Goldfish?" Jane said when we came home. "Goldfish? Have you gone mad?" I tentatively suggested they might be nice for the children. "Just so long as you know who's cleaning them..."

Tom's goldfish was small and quite nippy. "Speedy" seemed a fine name. Jessica's was altogether rounder: clearly it had not been at the back of the queue when the fishy flakes were handed out. "Bunter?" I suggested. "Porky? Going Large?"

"Biggy," proclaimed Jessica defiantly. So Speedy and Biggy it was, and they sat happily on top of the microwave. Cleo the cat sat next to them, watching, waiting – and wondering why we were taking so long to feed them to her.

Anyway, if the RSPCA want to take me in now, I'll come quietly. Cleaning out Speedy and Biggy was not my strong point. I did delegate it to Tom and Jess once, but after I'd pulled the washing machine out to mop up the flood it seemed simpler to do it myself. Gradually the water would turn darker and darker green until the poor fish were swimming round in some sort of primordial soup and I couldn't stand it any longer.

The bit I hated most was putting my hand into the slime to get their toys – the bridge and the diver and all the other junk we imagine makes a goldfish happy. One day I felt something new down there. I sighed, stuck my hand in again and pulled out Ben's long lost Lara Croft. She might have been free with the cornflakes, but even Lara didn't deserve to spend six weeks in the green sludge.

Jane sent me a text message yesterday, just before we were due to collect the children from school. "Emergency. Come home. Kids OK." I was baffled – if the kids were OK, what could be an emergency? She told me as I walked through the door. "The goldfish are dead."

"Dead?" I said stupidly. "What do you mean dead?"

"I mean," she said patiently, "That they are floating on their sides in that special way goldfish have of telling you that they are dead."

"Listen, children," I said twenty minutes later, trying to strike the right balance between seriousness and they-were-only-goldfish-after-all. "Mummy and Daddy, have some bad news…"

"Aaagghh!" screamed Jessica, "You haven't bought any chocolate. I hate you!"

No, we said, it was a bit more serious than that.

"Daddy," said Ben, "Are you going to put them in a hole in the garden?" If I have to, I thought wearily.

Fortunately Jane had a brainwave. "They're water animals," she told Ben. "They have a special watery Heaven."

"Where is it, Mummy?"

"In the sea, darling."

"How do they get there, Mummy?"

"If we put them down the toilet and say a magic prayer, their spirits will swim there."

"Alright, Mummy."

I tell you, sometimes the woman is a genius.

We trooped upstairs, and solemnly gathered round the toilet. Cleo followed, sensing her moment had come at last. Speedy and Biggy, entombed in tissue paper, were placed in the water. A magic prayer was duly intoned, and the children sadly flushed the toilet. Judging by her disgusted expression, Cleo saw it as a seriously wasted opportunity...

The Single Parent

Jane left me a few days ago. No, I couldn't believe it either. Just because her Mother was having a birthday ending in a zero she upped and left. Thursday afternoon, gone for three days, just like that.

"I'm off," she said. "See you Sunday night. Have fun." And she jumped into her car, collected her Mother and drove to a hotel. I mean, given the choice between a weekend of pampering, pedicures and peace and quiet – or one spent looking after me and the kids, what would you choose? I'll never understand women...

So there I was, a single parent for the weekend. Well, not strictly – unless my wife is reading this. Tom was on a football course all day Saturday, and Jessica decided to visit her Gran, so Ben and I had a lovely day. He played quietly with his soldiers, I watched the sport on telly and thought I was coping with it all pretty well.

Unfortunately a small riot broke out within five minutes of the children being back together, but I bribed my way to peace and harmony with 'film night.' Rent a video (*Spy Kids* never fails), push the settees up and open the largest packet of sweets the corner shop sells. Your dentist may not approve, but when your wife's abandoned you on Saturday night it takes some beating.

Today, though, has been an altogether different kettle of fish – or tin of puddings to be more precise. Granny was aiding and abetting my wife by being out all day, there was no football course, and to my horror the kids demanded Yorkshire Puddings with their lunch.

"You mean you want proper Sunday lunch?"

"Yes, we do," the committee replied. "Just like Mum makes – with Yorkshire Puddings."

Now I'm not a bad cook, just as long as it's all in one pan – stew, bolognese sauce, that sort of thing. But I have never made Yorkshire Puddings and I'm getting too old to be bothered with recipes. I was though, dimly aware that it was now possible to buy 'cheat' Yorkshire puds. This was duly confirmed in Tesco's freezer section. A nice old lady on the box promised that all I had to do was stick them in the oven, zap it to number seven, wait twenty five minutes and hey presto! Perfect Yorkshires and Dad's a hero.

Sadly, I now know that you're not supposed to keep opening the oven door and looking at them. It's also probably a good idea if the children don't flood the bathroom making you rush upstairs when there's a minute to go. What's more, I strongly suspect that the nice, smiling old lady is a serial liar. The children were not impressed by the small, black cricket balls I offered them. "It's traditional," I said. "They're supposed to be crispy."

"They're burnt," said Tom.

"No they're not," Jessica replied. "He's incinerated them."

You've probably realised by now that I'm not much of a new man. In addition to failing with the Yorkshires, you may as well know that while Jane's been away I have not done any cleaning. Nor have I washed any clothes, done any ironing, been shopping (except for beer, sweets and the hapless Yorkshires), changed the beds or got anything ready for school tomorrow.

Despite that, I'm exhausted. It's hard work running a home. Jane's due back in half an hour, but if she's feeling rejuvenated and fancies her chances tonight that's too bad. I'm pretty sure I'm getting a headache…

Monday's Swimming, Tuesday's Chaos

Once upon a time I had a job that involved seeing people in the evenings. Diary open and pen poised I'd phone them to make an appointment. "Probably Tuesday or Thursday would be best for me."

At that point there was always a sharp intake of breath on the other end of the phone. "Oh no," they'd reply. "Tuesday's Brownies, and Thursday's football."

"How about Monday then? I could probably manage that…"

"No, no, Monday's swimming."

"Right, well, let's see…if I re-arranged a few things, how does Wednesday sound?"

"That's ballet."

"Friday?"

"You're joking aren't you? We're too tired to do anything at all on Friday."

I'd then turn to my girlfriend and ask who was in charge of these people's lives. Why couldn't they sort themselves out? What sort of pathetic life were they living?

Many years on, I now know the answers, and let me confess that I'm not in control of my own life and no, we can't sort ourselves out and yes, by Friday we are absolutely cream crackered. What sort of pathetic life was it? Just normal family life, that's all.

The trouble is that Mitch Cook (football) and Susan Richards (ballet) – I'm pretty sure it's that way round – don't talk to each other. If they could just get together and agree that football courses would run from say, 9am to 11am, and ballet would be from 11:30 to 1:30 you'd hear the collective sigh of relief twenty miles away. Like other parents who drank too much red wine one night and carelessly had children of different sexes, we spend Saturday morning zig-zagging wildly across town, dropping off at Raincliffe (football), rushing to the YMCA (ballet), collecting one, collecting the other, and trying to find time in between to buy some food. Co-ordinate your kids' activities? It would be easier to sort out the National Rail Network.

And this is before Ben reaches five. At which point, he tells us, he'd like to go to martial arts. ("Marsha Larts," he says. Sounds like a nice girl.) Then there'll be swimming lessons, more football and more chaos. I'm not bright enough to do the Maths, but there's probably some formula along the lines of $G = K \times A$ divided by P, where G is the amount of gin you drink each week, K the number of kids you have, A how many activities they do and P the almost non-existent chance of finding a parking space anywhere near the YMCA.

And yet a friend of ours has four children, and seems to cope pretty well. How does she do it? Simple, she's only had boys. That's the answer you see – boys or girls, it doesn't matter, just don't mix them up. You could then go on and on having children, gradually moving up from an ordinary family car to an estate to a people carrier to a second hand bus. You would arrive at the football course in whatever vehicle you're currently driving, and tip out any number of boys. Then you can have a little snooze in the back of the bus for an hour until it's time to load them all up and go home.

Of course, six or eight pairs of muddy boots, socks, shorts and shirts coming home might be a bit of a problem. But that's your own fault for drinking those extra bottles of red wine...

Where are Amnesty when you need them?

Tom is standing on my underpants. Ben's about to open the door while Jane is stark naked, and Jessica is wailing. You've guessed it – we're at the swimming pool, and we're in a family changing room.

Changing cell to be more precise: it measures seven feet by five feet. If a prisoner were put in here Amnesty International would go ballistic. You wouldn't be able to move for compensation lawyers. So why is it deemed adequate for a family of five to get changed in?

Jane usually has these matters well under control. One swimming bag for her and Jessica, one for Tom, and I take care of Ben. Three bags, three changing rooms, no hassle. But today there is a momentary lapse in our concentration and the kids pounce. "Come on, Mum and Dad, we've found a family one." Before we can protest they are inside and half undressed. Wearily we shuffle in after them. What follows is not for the faint hearted, and were it available on prescription would rapidly become a highly effective method of birth control.

Tom is changed in zero seconds flat and won't wait for anyone else. Ben has no interest in getting changed, but is fascinated by opening and closing the doors.

Jessica can't find her goggles and informs the whole pool. Jane hisses, "Never again," through tight lips, and I rummage around for a twenty or a pound or whatever it is the lockers take this week.

Finally we make it to the pool. The children charge off and we fall into the water after them. For an hour and a half you're up and down flumes, in the waves and on the slides. (No, we're not at the local pool, how did you guess?) The prospect of getting changed again almost fades away. But you can't put it off for ever – not quite in perfect harmony, the family eventually head back to the prison cell...

"Tom, will you please stop trailing that towel along the floor?"

"What do you mean you've left your goggles? Well go back and get them."

"Ben, wait until we're in the changing room before you take your trunks off."

"No, Jess, I don't know which bag your pants are in."

"Because everything's muddled up that's why."

"Tom, will you please help Ben?"

"I am not standing in your way, I am simply trying to get dry."

"Rub yourself, darling, if you just stand there we'll be here until Christmas."

"Well then you wouldn't get any presents would you? Father Christmas isn't going to look in the swimming pool."

"Because Rudolph doesn't know the way. Because your Mother's navigating. How should I know?"

"No, Tom, I have not got a Mars Bar."

"Maybe, but only if you help Ben get dressed."

"Right, are we finally all ready? Open the door, Tom."

"Ouch! That was my shin, Tom. Try the other door."

"At last…"

Despite all this we will have forgotten something. I speak as someone who once had to go back and confess that our family had misplaced a three foot plastic dolphin. Last time it was only the car keys. Let's look on the bright side though – with luck the kids will fall asleep on the way back, and my irritatingly damp groin will have dried out in about twenty miles. The trouble is, it's Sunday – there'll just be time to pop them in the bath when we get home…

Like Father, Like Son

On balance I'd quite like to go to Heaven. It's debatable whether I'll pass the entrance exam – answers written on my sleeve in Chemistry O-level and various other misdemeanours – and I worry about getting bored as well. I mean, once you've caught up with your relatives, and checked your school history project with William the Conqueror, just what do you do for the rest of eternity?

The point is though, I need to see my Dad again. I owe him an apology. Hopefully he's up there now, smiling to himself as slowly and surely I turn into him. Sadly, my Dad died before I became a father – he would have loved the children. What he would have loved even more would be hearing me confess, "Well, Dad, you were right on that one as well..."

When I was a teenager – a fairly revolting one I now realise – I was pretty merciless with my Dad. Mum worked on a Saturday morning so Dad did the shopping. He had this thing about Tesco – he had to be there when they opened at 8:30. I would go on and on about it. "Dad, they are not going to sell out of food at eight forty." "Dad, you might as well drive the delivery lorry you're there that early..."

What happens now if I go shopping on a Saturday morning? Who's one of the twelve sad people queuing in the rain, waiting for the doors to open? Whatever Jane says ("Perhaps you could get a job stacking the shelves, darling…") I simply cannot help it.

Here's another one. I'd be doing something – homework, watching TV, thinking about Angela Miller – and my Dad would speak to me. I'd hear him, but well, you know what teenagers are. So he'd turn to Mum and say, "The message hasn't got there yet." It really irritated me. I wouldn't reply and he'd say it again – until we fell out. So what do I do when Tom doesn't answer? I turn to Jane and say, "He's not receiving us." Then I say to Tom, "Hello? Planet Earth to Tom, come in Tom…"

Long ago, in a galaxy far, far away a famous father once hissed, "You cannot escape me. It is your destiny." That's beginning to sound about right to me…

It therefore goes without saying that I now ridicule the bands on Top of the Pops and bemoan the pathetic lack of basic skill in Premiership footballers. I have even turned to Jessica and shouted, "That's it. I've had enough. I don't care if it takes all day – you will sit there until you've eaten it." No! How could I? As a child I swore, I took a solemn oath, that when I was a parent I would never, ever, say those words.

And "Turn it down." When did I start saying that? My Dad's basic greeting when I was a teenager. "Turn it down, have you done your homework?" "Turn it down, how did your cricket go?" And yet I am now incapable of going into a room where my children are watching TV without saying "Turn it down." I must say it at least four times a day. It's fourteen years before Ben leaves home. That's 4 x 14 x 365. I am going to say "turn it down" over 20,000 times. Will it ever make a difference? No – so why bother? Because it is my destiny, that's why.

But when Tom the teenager is ridiculing me in a few years, I'll just smile quietly to myself. Then I'll ring Tesco and book his place in the queue...

Sports Day

I realised we must be getting close to Sports Day when a stray Frisbee hit me on the back of my head. "Sorry, Dad," Tom shouted. "I'm practising for Sports Day."

"Right," I said. "What are you in?"

"Discus – that's what I'm practising."

"I've noticed that – anything else?"

"Seventy five metres – and the shot putt."

"The shot putt…" I said, and made a mental note to double the buildings insurance.

Sports Day's like many things – fine if you've only got one child. Three, and you need a sophisticated computer programme to tell you what part of the playing field you're due in next. Is it Ben in the 'Getting Dressed' race? Jessica in the 800m? Or do we risk Tom and his deadly discus?

It turned out to be Ben first. I'd have thought that at his age a simple sprint would have been fine – but no, as usual, the youngest children have the most complicated races. Ben's first was the 'Cooking Race.' Run for a bit, put on a chef's hat, run a bit more, pick up a pan, run, put the vegetables in, don't forget the wooden spoon, then sprint for the line. Only the wooden spoon to go and Ben was well in the lead. "Go on, Ben," I yelled. "GO ON!" Poor Ben was so startled he dropped the veg, forgot the spoon and

31

finished third. "It's the taking part at their age," Jane gently reminded me. Never mind, he redeemed himself with a gold medal in the Frog Jumping race – now there's an event to spice up London's bid for 2012.

With a bit of sprinting ourselves we managed to cram most things in, but what a good Sports Day really needs is a bit more time. And on balance I think I'd vote for a beer tent and a bookies as well. Not that some parents need the amber nectar to get over-excited, and judging by the encouragement there might have been a few side wagers struck. I strongly suspect Petra's Dad landed a major gamble in the infant sack race.

So there you are, it's a sunny day, you're nice and relaxed, your children are doing pretty well – and then someone mentions the Fathers' race. Not that your children let you forget. "Come on, Dad, you didn't do it last year either. Sean's Dad's doing it and he's way fatter than you…" Just for once though, I've got my sensible head on. I trained for it a couple of years ago and it took me a month to recover.

I was having my annual jog on the sea front – having waited three weeks for a day when the wind wasn't coming from Siberia – and I was going quite well. "Sports Day next week," I thought. "What about the Fathers' race? That'll impress the kids." I upped the tempo – visions of the children's faces as I streaked clear of the other Dads flashed in front of me. "Sprint!" I yelled at the top of my voice and hurtled past a terrified dog.

Suddenly a dreadful pain shot down the back of my left leg. I'd torn a hamstring and had to be helped back to my car by two old ladies. One of them looked at me shrewdly. "You know, dear," she said. "I don't think you're quite as young as you think you are."

These days I'm not even fit enough to go running with Jessica – but judging by her stunning performance in the 800m that's no disgrace. Maybe I'll just visit the online bookie and see what price she is for the 2016 Olympics...

I could have been James Bond

We finally made it on Sunday. About four years after Jane decreed that the children were now old enough and Sunday lunch was therefore an Official Family Meal – and about three years and ten months after I would have given up on it – the moment finally arrived. The children behaved themselves, we had a lovely meal, no-one argued, threw their food, spilt their drinks or did anything else to send my blood pressure into the stratosphere.

For once I was relaxed – which in my case means I drank far too much red wine, ate too many Yorkshire Puddings, and then waddled down to the corner shop for a large tub of premium ice-cream. "I'll have the 'tight-fitting trousers' flavour, please."

Eventually everything was shovelled into the dishwasher, and I collapsed on the sofa. I felt in the mood for a film, and with some subtle manipulation of his brother and sister, Tom persuaded us to watch James Bond.

Die Another Day? Tomorrow Never Dies? I can't tell them apart myself – it was the one where he ends up with the Chinese girl. I'm more of a Halle Berry man myself, but I doubt if the feeling's reciprocated.

As I watched James go through his paces, I shared a bit of useful information with the children.

"He's older than me…"

"Who?"

"James Bond – well, the actor that plays James Bond."

"No, he isn't."

"Honestly, he is. Not by much, but he's definitely older than me."

I could have left it there and not heard any more about it, but thanks to the red wine I started to dig a hole…

"I could have been James Bond you know, but I gave it up to be a Dad."

"Dad you are no way James Bond. No way…"

"Yeah, they asked me to audition, really."

"Dad…" (Tom has developed this way of saying 'Dad' which means "That's a stupid thing to say, Dad, and I'm now old enough to answer back…")

"Well, why not?" I said, digging deeper.

"Number one," said Tom, delivering a vicious poke to the place where I might once have had a six pack, "James Bond doesn't have this."

"And," said Jessica, not going to be left out of the blood sport, "His hair's not going grey."

"And he doesn't wear glasses to read the paper…"

"And he's not married to Mummy," Jessica finished, neatly skewering us both in one sentence.

Not so long ago I was a hero to my eldest two children. I must have missed the day it changed.

Suddenly they are aware that I don't have the coolest car at school, and that I don't drive as fast as teenage boys (but who does?) Jamie Clark's Dad is definitely better at football, and Harry's Dad – as I'm continuously reminded – is infinitely richer.

If you are still in that wonderful stage where your children think you are a combination of David Beckham, Michael Schumacher and Bill Gates, enjoy it while you can. Reality bites all too quickly and all too painfully.

Jane and I were going through some old photos last night. We found one of me on our honeymoon. Heaven knows what trick of the light had caused it but there I was – a beach God staring ruggedly at the camera, a bronzed hunk emerging from the Caribbean.

"Look at that bloke," I said to her. "I wonder what happened to him…"

Jane looked at me in my track suit bottoms, flip-flops and faded rugby shirt. "Who knows," she said. "He won't look like that now. The poor sod's probably had children…"

The Desperate Shelf

Members of the Salvation Army should look away now. We call it "The Desperate Shelf." Every home has one, and ours is on the bookcase between the novels and a shelf which – thanks to Auntie Jean's Christmas presents – holds three tablecloths Jane will only use if she suddenly goes colour-blind.

At the moment the Desperate Shelf contains two and half bottles of whisky (we don't drink whisky), half a bottle of Ouzo (Greece 1998), most of a bottle of Vodka (brought by Jane when she moved in with me twelve years ago), half a bottle of Tia Maria (did I once like that?) and several assorted liqueurs from various holidays – banana, strawberry, sun tan lotion flavour, the usual mixture.

Why we don't just throw the whole lot away or give it to our alcoholic friends I don't know. We need the space – ideally for books, but probably for more tablecloths. The trouble is there are times – and today is one of them – when we need the Desperate Shelf even more. All nine planets are in line and the necessary conditions have been met – specifically:

- The kids have driven us mad and we need a drink
- We've run out of beer, lager and gin

- The wine we opened on Sunday has turned to vinegar
- It's pouring down, so I refuse to go to the corner shop

Accordingly the Desperate Shelf has been declared open, and I'm drinking twelve year old vodka – although it could be four star petrol, there can't be much difference. Jane is torn between developing a taste for whisky and the sun tan flavour liqueur.

I once heard gin referred to as 'Mother's little helper', and I didn't know what people were talking about. We did have the occasional drink when we only had Tom, but certainly not until he was in bed. When Jessica arrived we bent the rule slightly and six o'clock became the watershed (or gin-shed in my wife's case). When Ben was born we threw the rule book out of the window and declared open house.

I filled in a form the other week which asked how many units of alcohol I drank. Why don't they just ask how many children you've got? That's a much more accurate guide. I was applying for some life cover, so like everyone I said four to six a week – the real answer is probably two or three times that. But how does anyone raise children without the support of Messrs Carlsberg and Gordon? We could have a go, but the only beneficiaries would be the divorce lawyers.

And if the answers from Ben's last birthday party are anything to go by we're not alone. "I like fizzy orange best," Emily told me, "But Mummy likes gin. She gets a new bottle every week." You can always rely on a four year old for the truth.

Of course, every time your children go to a party it works in reverse and you risk them revealing your deepest secrets, but I'm pretty sure ours haven't realised the significance of the Desperate Shelf yet.

A few years though and Tom and his teenage mates will discover it. We'll relent, let them have a party and that'll be the end of the Desperate Shelf – and the carpet, probably.

I'm still not ready for the thought of teenage boys in the house. I'd better have another glass of this twelve year old four star to prepare myself. Between you and me, it's not bad once you develop a taste for it...

Front Door Tax

If I live in a house I pay council tax: if I earn anything I pay income tax, and if I buy anything I pay value added tax. And you know what? Now I'm a Dad I pay Front Door Tax.

You may not know it by that name, but rest assured, if you're a Dad, you'll certainly be paying it. This is how it works. You're just about ready to go out in the morning. Car keys in hand, you make for the door. Then they hit you with the tax demand...

"Ben got his ten metre swimming badge, yesterday. He needs £1.20 to pay for it."

"Dad, we're going on our field trip today. Mr. Phillips says we can take five pounds for spending money."

"Yes, Daddy. And Mrs. Clark says we have to bring in three pounds for the farm trip..."

"Darling... I don't seem to have any change. Lend me two pounds for a sandwich, will you?"

Eleven pounds twenty to walk out of your own front door. Times by five, times by how ever many weeks there are in a school year – on second thoughts don't bother. And it's not just school days – Saturday was particularly savage: a new football shirt for Tom (he must play for the only under tens in the country who change their strip more often than Manchester

United), Jessica needed something for Brownies, Jane needed change for the car park... "Oh, and Ben's got two parties this weekend – have you got ten pounds for presents?" So when Tom came in and informed me that Harry's Dad had just bought a new car and "It's way better than yours, Dad," something snapped.

"Just-sit-there-and-listen-to-me," I hissed. "Number one, Harry is an only child. Number two he does not eat a truckload of chocolate every day and number three he seems to play no sport whatsoever."

"But..." said Tom.

"But nothing!" I yelled. "If I didn't have children I'd drive a Ferrari. Your mother would drive a Ferrari and without your ever-changing football shirts I could even buy your damn Granny a Ferrari." A slight exaggeration perhaps, but you see my point.

Every Friday I go to the cashpoint and extract what I think will comfortably be enough for the weekend. Every Monday morning I survey the surviving wreckage of copper and the odd twenty pence. What does it add up to? Another week of corned beef sandwiches for Dad, that's what.

Jane told me this morning that Ben is starting a 'Little Ninjas' martial arts course. That's a double whammy – Front Door Tax to pay for it and then come home and kick Dad to show him what you've learned.

Now he has a child it can only be a matter of time before Gordon Brown catches on to the potential of Front Door Tax and it becomes official Government policy. "My sandwich money?" Jane will ask as I go out. "Oh, and the Inland Revenue left this little envelope for your small change..." I suppose there is one consolation though – at least with four children, Tony Blair will have to fork out more FDT than I do.

So there you are – if you want to get rich, don't have children. What's more, as you're reading this, we'll be singing *Happy Birthday* to Tom – ten today. With the teenager already lurking in the shadows, the tax demands can only increase. But I wouldn't change a thing. Don't tell the kids, but they'd be a bargain at five times the cost...

The Curious Case of the Missing Shoe

I was sitting peacefully at my desk when Jane phoned. "Have you got Tom's shoe?" she demanded.

"What? I'm at work…"

"Well you're no damn use are you?" she said, and slammed the phone down.

She called back an hour later. She hadn't calmed down. "He's had to go to school in trainers."

"Why?"

"Because he's lost his shoe, that's why."

"What do you mean he's lost his shoe?" Sometimes I'm not very bright where domestic matters are concerned.

"The shoe which goes on his foot," she said. "Your son has lost it. I have spent all morning looking for it."

Somehow he was always *my* son when he was in trouble. "OK, OK," I said.

"I've got to call in at lunchtime, I'll find it." My gentle wife then suggested that as I could rarely find my own clothes there was no chance of me finding Tom's – except that she didn't quite use those words…

Lunchtime – the key thing was to think like Tom. What would he do with his shoes? What any ten year

43

old would do – take them off without undoing the laces and leave them in the middle of the hall. So who else could be involved? Jessica – maybe they'd had an argument. Where would she put them? "Oh no," I said to myself, and started to go through the rubbish bin.

I'd just covered myself in yesterday's bacon fat when Jane walked in. "If you're hungry, dear, we keep the food in the fridge." Mrs. Sarcastic was still with us then. "Anyway, I've already done that."

"Let's think it through," I said. "Behind the computer desk?"

"Looked – four Mars Bar wrappers but no shoe."

"Under the TV?"

"Ben's toast."

"Jessica's bedroom?"

"She says not – besides, it's so untidy I can't get the door open." I was fired and DCI Jane took over the investigation. "You're sure he'd got his shoe on when you came home?"

I'd collected all three of them yesterday. Surely I couldn't have missed Tom walking into the house with only one shoe on? He'd spent the entire journey home fighting with Ben so he'd certainly had my full attention. "Absolutely," I said. "He came in, took his shoes off and dropped his blazer on the floor." Just like he did every day.

I walked into the lounge and looked behind the settee. And there it was. "Jane… it's here."

"Where?"

"Behind the settee."

"That's the other one – he threw it there this morning."

"The other one?"

"Yes, dear. You may not know it because you never buy them, but Tom wears two shoes." Jane fixed me with an uncompromising stare. "I am seriously fed up with this. The only place it can be is in your car."

We weren't very far from an argument now – typical really, the children lose their clothes so the parents have a fight. "I was at work. How can it be in my car?"

"Because you brought them home."

"For the last time, Jane – Ben and Tom were in the back of the car, they were fighting, Ben attacked Tom and…" Something awful flashed through my memory. "And pulled his shoe off," I finished pathetically. I hadn't seen the shoeless Tom walk in because I'd been carting Ben straight up to his bedroom. I slunk out to the car – the shoe was on the back seat. I tamely presented it to Jane.

"I rest my case," she said triumphantly. Oh well, she'll only remind me of it every day for the next twenty years…

Going Underground

For the last two years we've held Tom's birthday party in a cave. It was a week late this year due to school re-arranging half term, but nothing can disrupt Tom's routine. The remorseless nagging to make sure I've booked it, the assiduous practice on the computer, planning his tactics – and then the day itself. We meet six of his friends at the local cyber café and I say a sad farewell to the daylight. The boys rush down into the gloom to bomb each other into oblivion for two hours, seven of them huddled over computer screens, re-fuelled by fizzy drinks and chocolate, muttering "This nuclear bomb is way wicked."

Normally my role in all this – with help from Jessica – is to maintain a steady supply of strawberry pop and Yorkie bars, collect the wrappers and stop them hearing what the teenagers next to them are saying. Not this year: Harry has been sick all night and can't come. They're playing *Red Alert* and Tom's plans call for two teams of four. The game cannot go on without North Korea. A substitute is needed, and it's me: the fact that I don't know how to play is irrelevant. As far as Tom's concerned it's ideal – as all fathers will confirm, ten year old boys never tell you the rules until after they've thrashed you.

My battle station is in the corner under the stairs.

I'm shoehorned into the sort of space beloved by medieval torturers – not big enough to stand up, impossible to sit down comfortably.

The game begins – it's the usual strategy: build up your armies and then unleash hell. As no-one will tell me what the controls are I do not build up my defences quickly enough. The inevitable squadron of B52 bombers rapidly appears on my radar. Before I can ask for help, they've nuked me back to the stone age. I watch the battle unfold for the next fifteen minutes, until – entirely according to plan – "You are Victorious!" appears on Tom's screen.

And then tragedy. The server crashes. Perhaps Bill Gates has taken pity on me. But the sixteen year old genius in charge of these things soon announces that he's fixed it. "Sort of," he says, "It'll only play *Counter Strike.*"

"Yesssss!!" scream seven would be assassins.

I groan silently. *Counter Strike* is my nemesis. Terrorist, counter-terrorist, SAS or Arctic Commando – it makes no difference which one I choose, pretty soon my blood will be splattered all over the screen. Once you're past forty that's it – reaction time thirty minutes when it needs to be thirty milliseconds. When I've been eliminated first for six games in a row I give up and let Jessica take over. She immediately shows an aptitude for this type of work by convincing a 10 year old terrorist that she's on his side, and then shooting him in the back. That's my girl...

It gradually dawns on Tom that the survival of his elite unit may depend on his sister's skill with an AK47. Perhaps I'll be able to go back to Jane and report a thaw in the sibling cold war.

The minutes pass slowly as I sit on the stairs watching the carnage unfold. The body count eventually exceeds the Yorkie bar count. But finally the time runs out, and the boys are led blinking back into the sunlight.

"Something different next time, Tom?" I suggest.

"No way," they all chorus. They're already making plans for next year. Still, that gives me twelve months to practice – or to sign a treaty with Jessica...

The Unkindest Cut

Jane and I took a long time deciding whether to stick or twist. We'd two lovely children, they were healthy, we were already exhausted – surely that was enough? But there was this nagging feeling – maybe just one more…

In the end we let nature and red wine take its course. The problem with children is that they're expensive toys. The bottle of Aussie aphrodisiac that led to Ben might have had £4.99 on the label, but the bill so far is just a little bit North of that.

Much as we love them we can't afford any more, so our conversations of late have tended towards contraception in general, and my vasectomy in particular. In Jane's opinion they should have tended towards it a lot sooner, but I've become pretty expert at avoiding the subject. "I'd love to discuss it, darling, but isn't ER due to start?"

Not that I'm frightened, you understand – but when Jane was first pregnant we did the ante-natal course. This included a tour of the relevant part of the hospital. I glanced into one room and saw an especially ancient nurse. Her eyes burned in the way you sometimes see in pictures of religious fanatics. I noticed that her hands were shaking.

"What happens in there?" I asked.

"Vasectomies," was the reply. "You won't need to worry about that just yet."

To be honest, I've worried about very little else for the last ten years. Every time Jane mentioned the subject all I could see were those staring eyes and shaking hands. As I kept telling her, I just don't think the time's quite right.

Unfortunately Jane does, and she finally pinned me down last week. She convinced me that Nurse Scissorhands would now be safely retired and two days later my GP was running through the standard questions:

"You're sure you don't want any more children?"

"No thanks," I said, showing him a bank statement.

"Supposing anything happens to Jane?"

"I should be alright," I replied. "She's got plenty of life cover."

But all this was irrelevant compared to my main question. "How long's the waiting list?"

"About six months."

"Oh dear," I said. I'd been hoping for three years.

"You could always go privately," he suggested, and before I could stop him he scribbled down the number of the Marie Stopes clinic and pushed it into my hand.

Jane seized on this with enthusiasm when I got home. "Are you going to ring them?" she demanded.

"Well…"

"You should, now you've made your mind up." I wasn't aware that I had made my mind up, but obviously Jane had. I called this morning. The phone was briskly answered by Nurse Cashandcut.

She quoted a price. It seemed expensive compared to a new set of golf clubs or a season ticket to watch 'Pools. On the other hand compared to six months flak from Jane it was amazing value.

"So when could you do it?" I asked, hopefully staring at the 'next year's appointments' section of my diary.

"Next Thursday," she said. "Two o'clock or three thirty."

I gulped. "That's rather sudden."

"We get a lot of cancellations," she said. "Some men get cold feet."

It wasn't my feet I was worrying about. "Really?" I said. "I'll just discuss it with my wife. She may not think the time's quite right."

I quickly put the phone down. And now if you'll excuse me I need an hour in a darkened room, while I work out what I'm going to say to Jane...

Does it really matter?

I want to go on holiday. There are four weeks left of the school term and I've had enough. Jessica has fallen out with her best friend, Tom hasn't been picked for the football team and Miss Grayson has told Ben off for the first time. The children are miserable, it's dark at three o'clock, and my stress level is off the scale. It is not helped by the fact that I have to repeat everything I say twenty-six times.

Regular readers will know that I expect to say "Turn it down" around 20,000 times before the children leave home, but why stop there? You're not a parent if you haven't said:

- It's time to finish on the computer
- Sit properly at the table, will you?
- You're tidying your bedroom – and that's final
- For God's sake stop fighting
- Don't stand on the new settee

My current refrain is "Stop swinging on the door handle." Jessica is an intelligent girl. Why can't she realise that telling her to stop using the door handle as a piece of gym equipment means for ever, not just for the next five seconds?

But don't assume that I only say negative things to the kids. I could be American I'm so positive at times.

"Go for it! Give it your best shot." And my favourite – courtesy of Tom Hanks' Mum, (sorry, Mom) in *Philadelphia* – "We're not raising our children to sit at the back of the bus."

Then there's my accumulated wisdom. "Why is it cheap, Jessica? Because it's no damn good." And one that Tom may well learn painfully one day – if it seems too good to be true it is too good to be true.

But does anything your parents say make any difference? Is it worth me setting a world blood pressure record persuading Tom to finish his shoot-em-up game, when I know I'll be saying the same thing tomorrow? Why don't I just accept that my dinner will taste better if it's eaten to the screams of freshly slaughtered aliens?

Of all the things my parents said to me, which ones do I really remember? The daft ones.

"Don't leave your jeans on the bedroom floor," my Dad once told me. When I asked why he said, "Well, if there's a fire in the night, you might trip over your jeans and not be able to escape." Even Dad must have known that was ridiculous. I couldn't sleep for trying to work out the odds on such an unlikely double. The trouble is, I'm now capable of exactly the same stupidity.

"Don't leave your Game Boy on the window ledge."

"Why not?"

"Well, if there's a flood in the middle of the night it could get washed out of the window…"

So what will they remember me for? Come the day when I'm just a photo on the mantelpiece will Tom turn to his wife and say, "You know, honey, thanks to my Dad's wisdom I made the right decision there." Or will he say, "My Dad? Once told me how to save my Game Boy from a flood – that's about all, I think."

So why don't I admit defeat and say, "OK, Tom, your bedroom's a tip, but it's your tip and I'm sure your school uniform's in there somewhere." I don't say it because I'm married to Jane, but I'd quite like to try the experiment. Mind you she'll have to be away for a month or so. It might work. Then again I might have to call in a UN taskforce to tidy up before she comes home...

Best Laid Plans...

I was trying not to smile, but I had to go on a business trip. Regrettably I would be away overnight. In a hotel... with a lovely big swimming pool, a peaceful bar and a large fried breakfast. Some careful juggling of my schedule ensured that I didn't have to see anyone until lunchtime. The wonderful prospect of peace and quiet and a morning off was within touching distance.

"You look like you're packing for your holidays." Jane seemed less than convinced that two pairs of swimming trunks were necessary for a business meeting.

"You wouldn't want me to put weight on, dear," I said.

Two hours later I arrived at the hotel. I was met by a sign at reception – 'Swimming Pool Closed.' Apparently it was due to what they termed a 'chemical imbalance.' I suppose that's a technical term for what children do in swimming pools. They faithfully promised me that the pool would be open at seven the next morning. I could live with that. I was tired from the journey and it seemed a sensible compromise to replace one swim with two beers. I duly drank my beer, ate a sandwich, and went to sleep. I'd set the alarm on the mobile for six-thirty so I could be first in the pool – complete with freshly balanced chemicals – and then eat a prodigiously large breakfast.

The phone rang – six-thirty already? I'd hardly been asleep. I managed to silence it after some fumbling and blearily looked at the clock. 4:32 blinked back at me. Oh God, an emergency at home. I checked the number that had rung – perhaps Jane had phoned me from the hospital? 'No number' the phone said. I shan't tell you what I said. Junk phone calls, at four-thirty in the morning. Needless to say I couldn't get back to sleep.

At seven I trooped down to the pool. No sign on reception as I passed so presumably the chemicals were back in harmony. "Sorry, sir," an unhealthy looking health club attendant said. "Pool's closed."

"What for?" I said.

"Chemical imbalance, sir. We've sent for a man."

"Where from?"

"Swindon, sir."

"That's two hundred miles away."

"Yes, sir."

I trudged back to my room and contemplated what now seemed to be an interminable morning stretching in front of me. I phoned home – at least the children would be in a good mood. It was a non-uniform day at school in aid of Children in Need – I'd paid the £3 Front Door Tax as I left. Jessica answered.

"Hello, darling."

"Mummy has been horrid to me."

"What's the matter?"

"She's making me wear an itchy top." When the mood takes her, all Jessica's tops are itchy. Tom was no better.

"Mummy's being grumpy. She won't let me wear my favourite jumper."

"Why not?" I asked Jane.

"Because your child has poured Coco Pops down it, that's why." Ben, meanwhile, wailed steadily in the background. I told Jane about the swimming pool and the early morning alarm call. She didn't seem inclined to sympathise.

No swim, no sleep and a riot at home. At least you could rely on the traditional English breakfast – I ordered everything, plus extra black pudding. I put down the newspaper, picked up my knife and fork, took a deep breath and – the mobile rang. It was Jane. "I can't talk now, darling," I said. "I'm with some clients."

"Who's that then?" she said, "Mr. Bacon and Mr. Egg? You wouldn't want to put weight on, dear." There's no escape is there? The wretched woman has spies everywhere...

Dear Santa

Three weeks, two days, twelve hours and seventeen minutes. Ask Tom or Jessica at any moment of the day and they will give you a precise countdown to six o'clock on Christmas morning. They've turned into festive versions of the Speaking Clock. Ben still measures time in 'sleeps' but the Advent calendars are out now, so even he can see the finishing line.

The children have responded to the first chocolate to drop out of Hogwarts by re-doubling their efforts. I don't know how the postman at the North Pole is coping, but down here we're in serious trouble. A new Christmas List arrives every day. Thanks to Mr. Pettitt's IT class, Tom's is on permanent display as the screen saver.

He wants an 'exploder' for his Game Boy — what on earth is that? If it's a self-destruct device that blows it up after I've heard that wretched tune non-stop for two hours then he can have six of them, but I doubt it. Other than that Tom's list consists of large chunks of computer wizardry copied from very fat magazines. The only thing I can understand is the prices and they're way too high.

Ben's approach is much simpler. If he sees a toy he wants it. The fact that his bedroom carpet hasn't been sighted for three weeks is immaterial. He stumbled across an Argos catalogue the other day. "I've found something I want, Daddy," he said, dragging the book towards me.

"What's that?" I asked.

"These, Daddy," he said, with pages 1107-1142 grasped between his fingers. And that's before he's seen *Lord of the Rings 3*...

Only Jessica injects a note of realism – it's just expensive realism. Give her credit, she's the only one to actually include a book on her list – but sadly item six is simply "money," followed by brackets containing a single word: "lots."

But one thing our children don't do is snoop on their Christmas presents. When I was a child I went to any lengths to find out what I'd been bought. Mum would regularly come home to find my feet poking out from under the bed, and on Christmas morning all my presents had torn wrapping paper. Mind you, when you've sent your parents a specific list (plus duplicate copy to Santa just in case), you can dispense with all that undignified crawling around, and devote your full attention to the Advent calendar.

The serious news is that Jane is now pestering me for my list. Secretly I think she wants to be one of those dreadful people who have all their presents wrapped by July. The prezzies then spend so long under the bed that they come out on Christmas morning encased in cobwebs. Like most men though, Christmas doesn't appear on my radar screen until the dates in December begin with a '2'. I did astonish myself earlier this year when I bought Jane a Christmas present in October. "I've finally got it sorted this year,"

Mr. Smug told everyone. Needless to say I haven't bought anything since and I can't remember where I've put the one present I did buy. It's 'in a safe place' somewhere – no doubt I'll find it around August next year.

But list? What list? I'd like some new golf clubs and a new laptop, but I rather think Jane is looking for words more like 'shirt' and 'book'. She's starting to get a bit cross with me. To be blunt, she's threatening to hit me with the Argos catalogue. Suddenly doing my list looks like a good idea – and a self-defence manual might be the first thing on it...

The Gentle Maiden

The School Nativity Play – the sort of event that makes you think the only worthwhile career is selling camcorders.

Ben's a shepherd this year. He was a shepherd last year as well, except that he was a very sick shepherd and missed it. As the whole nursery class were shepherds it wasn't crucial.

Over the years we've managed to avoid our kids being trees or sheep or snowflakes. I know you're not supposed to admit it these days, but I want my children to be Mary or Joseph. King Herod and the Angel Gabriel will also do. I have a friend who is a seriously over-ambitious parent. One year his son landed the part of a rock – how did he cope with that? More to the point though – how did his wife make the costume?

Jane is now something of an expert in this department, and doesn't regard a shepherd as more than ten minutes work. Tea towel round his head, something to tie it on with, scruffiest cloak in the dressing up box, sandals from last summer and Ben's your shepherd.

The not-very-much-missed Mrs. Allsopp still holds a special place in Jane's list of villains for the letter she sent home when Tom was a king. "Tom has been chosen to play a king this year," it said. "He requires a long tunic in purple or navy, a cloak (which should shimmer), and a gold crown. He also needs a telescope and a brightly wrapped present." Rumours that Mrs. Allsopp was trying to sell the Nativity Play to Twentieth Century Fox never entirely went away. Fortunately Mrs. Allsopp did.

The real stress came a couple of years ago – Jessica was chosen to play Mary. Yes, Little Miss Volatile was cast as the gentle maiden, meek and mild. She came home and proudly produced a piece of paper from her school bag. "These are my lines," she announced. "We need to practice."

Owing to the non-availability of Tom (emptying the biscuit tin into himself), Ben (emptying something else on to his bedroom floor) and Jane (emptying the gin bottle I shouldn't wonder), I was cast as the innkeeper.

The Blessed Virgin placed me at the bottom of the stairs and issued my instructions. "Now when I knock, you pretend to open the door and say 'no room.'"

"No room?" I asked

"Not like that." She looked at me patiently. "Like this," she said, and bellowed "No room" at the top of her voice.

"Right, darling," I said. It seemed the simplest option

"Then I say, 'We are very tired. We have travelled through night and day' and you say, 'Hard Luck.'"

"Hard Luck?"

Jessica gave me the withering look Jane reserves for slugs caught eating her plants. "Daddy you are not very good at this are you? Not 'hard luck' – like this…" They probably heard her in Bethlehem. "Then Joseph says something and you say, 'Alright then, you can sleep in the stable round the back.'"

I have to say that I was so entranced by the sight of my daughter as actor/director that I didn't really concentrate on learning my lines. This was a serious mistake. By take six I still wasn't word perfect, and the last I saw of the Gentle Maiden was her stomping off upstairs. I think I caught "Can't get anything right," just before her bedroom door slammed.

Fortunately Ben doesn't have any words this year, so I'm safe. Two years time though and I could be working with King Herod. I'd better get it right then – knowing Ben, he'll have a sword…

Christmas Crackers

I spent most of Christmas morning under the dining room table. This had nothing to do with Christmas Eve celebrations and everything to do with Frodo Baggins. Top of Ben's Christmas list were "*Lord of the Rings* men" – as if his bedroom didn't have enough "men." Never mind, by eight o'clock on Christmas Day we'd added Gandalf the White, Sam, a couple of baddies and Mister Frodo.

By eight-thirty Frodo's arm had fallen off. Ben burst into tears and I was sentenced to hard labour on my hands and knees until it was found. As Ben had been playing on the dining room table when the tragedy occurred, looking underneath it seemed the obvious answer. Not so – half an hour later Frodo was still one limb short, Ben was still wailing and tempers were fraying. We were just about to perform a strip search when the offending arm turned up in his dressing gown pocket. Determined there would be no repeat I went to my toolbox to dig out the superglue.

While I'm there I may as well find that very tiny Philips screwdriver as various toys need a combined total of around ninety-nine batteries. Given my singular lack of talent once the toolbox is in play, I'm delighted that I no longer have to fit plugs, but let's not stop there. It's time for manufacturers to put batteries in the box as well, and the screwdriver you'll need to fit them, and a smoker-style notice on the outside: "Superglue required in thirty minutes."

That's assuming you can actually get anything out of the box in the first place. Why is it that every toy you buy is now fastened in with more straps than you'd find at the bondage club Christmas party?

Jane meanwhile was building Ben's Robot Mutant Zoid. "Age 5 and above," it said on the box – just on the off chance you can find a five year old with a degree in mechanical engineering. My wife is an intelligent woman: she has professional qualifications – but her look of satisfaction when she finished the Zoid was something to behold. Her expression when I knocked it on the floor ten minutes later was not.

After Xmas dinner (not surprisingly slightly late) we finally admitted defeat and gave the kids a PS2. Five games of 'Gran Turismo' later I was having a serious crisis of confidence. As Tom hurtled round corners at 200 kph I bumped pathetically along the grass verge. Jessica treated me to her most condescending look and informed me I was "Way useless."

I shudder to think what will happen when Tom and his generation get behind the wheel of real cars. Will the roads be safer thanks to their PS2 honed reactions – or will they carry on as they do now? "Look, Dad – just crash into the wall like this and you bounce off in the right direction."

"What about the pedestrians you've just killed?"

"Don't worry – you don't lose any points." Unless you're a pedestrian that is.

Worse followed on Boxing Day when Granny arrived with a shoot-em-up. Swiftly cast in the role of James Bond's assistant, I walked straight into the swimming pool and drowned myself. Tom had obtained his normal head start by failing to explain the controls – even when he did though, I could no more find the enemy spies than I could find Frodo's arm.

At least there's some respite this afternoon. We're off to see if the real Frodo finally makes it to Mount Doom – and let's hope he's still got his arm after three and a half hours...

Snappers

When I was at school they were known as 'Snappers.' To Jessica and her friends they're now 'Fortune Tellies.' Whatever you call them, you'll definitely have made one. Take a square of paper and fold it so you get a diagonal cross. Now take the four corners and fold them into the middle of the square. Turn the paper over and do the same again. Now, fold your square in half – and then put your thumbs and forefingers into the little pockets you've just made and check that it 'snaps' properly. Satisfying isn't it? And instantly you're back in the school playground.

Now the real fun begins. On top of the flaps you used to write 'Red, green, blue, yellow,' and so on. Now you're a parent you may feel that 'Stress, worry, expense...' is more appropriate. Jessica is currently into animals. Every time I turn round there she is: "Come on, Daddy. Toad, frog, tiger or zebra?"

On the inside of the Snapper numbers one to eight usually appear. Then under the flaps you write – whatever you like. When I was at school our Snappers were an origami version of love-hearts. "Be mine," "You're sweet," "Let's hold hands," and so on. Like birthday cards, I suspect that Snappers are rather more direct these days. I once followed Angela Miller round the playground for two days with a Snapper I'd made just for her.

"Blue," she sighed when I finally cornered her.

"B-L-U-E," I chanted. "Two, three, six or eight?"

"Six," she said, then "Eight." I grinned at her.

"What's it say?" she demanded.

"Kiss me," I replied in triumph. It was Friday before she realised it said "Kiss me" under every flap. First thing Monday morning she marched straight up to me. I didn't bother choosing a colour. Just the expression on her face told me that every flap would say "Get lost."

Using the same principle I made one for Jessica. "Tidy your bedroom," it said. "Set the table," and so on. Jane was quite impressed by this new initiative in parenting. Sadly, my daughter proved to be a good deal less gullible than Angela. She was back ten minutes later with her reply – "Eat chocolate," "Ignore homework," and other flights of fancy.

Mind you, Snappers don't just have to be for children. I might well be able to use one to deflect Jane. Next time she tells me the door handle needs fixing I can turn to my Snapper. "Hang on, love – 'Pools, Toon, Roker or relegated?" As I'm a new man "do jobs" would obviously be an option – just not one that stood much chance.

And why not extend their use into sport? An awful lot of difficult decisions could become easier – even for the England manager.

Five months to Euro 2004 and the left side of midfield still isn't sorted. Stick with Heskey? Bring back Sinclair? Go north for Alan Thompson? Sven doesn't have to lose any sleep over it, all he needs is a Snapper. Jot down the eight possibilities under the flaps, then it's straightforward. "Right, Nancy," he could say over dinner. "Chelsea, Barca, Juventus or Man Utd?" A couple of numbers later his problems would be solved. Thinking back to some England performances you get the feeling the team really was chosen like that.

Meanwhile Jessica has turned up to haunt me again. Tom disagreed with number seven and has torn her Snapper in half. She gives me her best "twist-you-round-my-little-finger" look and tells me I'm "Way good at making Snappers." There – what more could a Dad want...

Snow Joke

There are days – and Monday to Friday are five of them – when it would be easier if Jessica left school now and went straight to university. Not that my eight year old has suddenly collected ten GCSEs or anything – it's just that her body clock is already on Student Time. Given the choice she would go to bed somewhere past midnight – and wake up around lunchtime. Jessica is to mornings what King Herod was to child welfare.

Through the week we haul her out of bed, stand her upright so she can get dressed, force food between her lips and tip her into the car. Most mornings she is just about conscious by the time she reaches school. The burden of this falls on Jane, who has to cope with it 90% of the time while I slope off to work early. If her job permitted, I have no doubt my wife would swap her nine o'clock coffee for something very much stronger.

Jessica is also bad tempered – I love my daughter greatly, but if losing your temper ever becomes a professional sport she'll make a fortune. Five years on, the thought of her with PMT is truly terrifying – please don't expect a column that week, as I plan to spend it on a barren rock off the coast of Scotland.

It all came to a head last Wednesday. Whatever the

original cause – probably a simple request to brush her hair – by the time they reached school my wife and daughter had reached DefCon 3, or whatever you call the stage two minutes before they pass George Dubya the briefcase. That night we sat Jessica down and had a Serious Talk with her – not just a talk, but a capital 'S' capital 'T' talk.

"And if that doesn't work," Jane said, "She can join a convent."

I wasn't hopeful – either of the talk working or of Jessica turning into Julie Andrews. I was certainly not prepared for a sweet voice saying, "Hello, Daddy," at seven fifteen the next morning. Hair brushed, ready for school, it was Jessica. "Can I help with breakfast?" she asked.

"Thank you, darling," I stammered – and then shot off to exchange high-fives with Jane.

Thirty seconds later our triumph was shattered. "It's closed!" screamed a voice from upstairs.

"What's closed?"

"School!" yelled Tom. "It's on the radio." I looked out of the window. OK, it had snowed, but cars were still going up and down the main road.

"I don't believe you," I said.

But fifteen minutes later we had to admit defeat. "Tough," I tell the children when they say, "It's not fair." "Life's not fair," I say. "Get used to it." But come on – Jane and I finally get Jessica sorted out and we are beaten by the school's first Snow Day in living memory. Not fair? Too damn right it wasn't.

Six hours later I am on top of a hill overlooking the North Sea. My feet are wet and the wind is straight

71

from Siberia. Far below me my daughter has just crashed off her sledge and somersaulted ten yards down the slope. Hopefully she's OK. I am too cold to have any stronger feelings.

All around me parents are pining for their nice warm offices. A quick poll confirms that none of us ever had a 'Snow Day.' Clearly headmasters in our day were made of sterner stuff. On the other hand Jessica's headmaster has a daughter of the same age – maybe he just needed a day off. Or maybe he's already somewhere off Scotland, hunting for his rock...

Mis-Spent Middle Age

I am eating humble pie – large portions of it. For as long as I can remember I have mercilessly mocked Jane's addiction to Reality TV programmes. *Big Brother*, *Fame Academy*, *Pop Idol* – I have wandered into the lounge and laughed at them all. I did cast an occasional eye over *I'm a Celebrity* last year, but only because I'm a cricket fan and knew about Phil Tufnell. As far as I could tell, my only interest in such programmes would be as a minder – making sure the children didn't watch them after nine o'clock.

Then last week I took Jane a drink whilst a treacle covered John Lydon was digging for stars and dodging ostriches. And I have been hooked ever since. Jane is not entirely delighted at this. She told me off the other day for never watching anything on TV with her, but she seems to have tired of my company during *Celeb* pretty quickly. This may be because I'm consistently offering advice – the man who nearly demolished the house trying to fix up Jessica's netball hoop sits there saying, "Why don't they build a fish trap?" "They could snare some snakes," and "I'd dig a pit and catch something."

Jane's patience snapped at this last one. "If you dug a pit," she said, "You'd forget where it was and fall in it yourself next morning."

She's still baffled as to why I'm so hooked on *Celeb*. Ditto the children can't quite understand how I've suddenly become an expert on texting. Where I once regarded "Big up 4 Kez lord b 2 go" as a foreign language, it's now a vital piece of inside information. Sadly, the main reason I'm addicted to *Celeb* is that you can back your opinions with hard cash. Once you've learned the language the regular flow of on-screen text messages are a fairly reliable guide and by the time you read this I'll hopefully be celebrating the victory of Queen Kerry.

The trouble is, I haven't told Jane about this. As the tension mounts it's becoming increasingly difficult to keep a straight face – and this time, it's absolutely crucial that Jane doesn't find out. She has a history of stealing my winnings.

About three seasons ago it was plainly obvious that Sunderland would win the North East mini-league. Boro were in decline and the Magpies needed rebuilding. Half way through the season I'd mentally spent my winnings on a new set of golf clubs. Two weeks before my eagerly-awaited pay day Jane and I were in town at lunchtime. Suddenly I spotted the bookie walking towards us. I desperately tried to steer Jane across the road, but it was too late. "Sunderland!" He shouted at me. "Clever lad! Everyone else backed Newcastle."

"What's he talking about?" Jane asked.

"Oh, er…just a friendly discussion," I stammered.

"That's a nice win for you," the fool continued.

"A nice win?" said Jane "And how much would that be?" She smiled sweetly at the wretched man, and can you believe it? He actually told her. So much for my golf clubs – five minutes later we were looking at washing machines.

This time it's going to be different. The bookies are on the internet now, and as long as I can control my emotions, Jane will remain in blissful ignorance. As Joey from Durham so neatly put it, "Go 4 it Kezza U R well fit girl!"

I can almost feel those new golf clubs in my hand. I just hope Jane understands "U R well fit" when she opens her Valentine's card...

One Short

We are missing a child. Tom is currently in France with the school choir. I will happily admit to a truly awful singing voice so when I heard that Tom was in the choir I very nearly demanded a paternity test. To be honest, he wasn't keen at first, as choir practice had an unfortunate knack of clashing with football. "Just stick with it for this week," we'd say every Tuesday.

Then rumours of a possible trip to France began to circulate. Tom started to waiver. The trip – and its detour to Disney – was eventually confirmed. "Never liked football anyway," he said.

So on Friday night Jane took him to school at midnight, bag in one hand, pillow in the other. According to Mr. Turner's schedule the coach would leave for Dover at 00:20 precisely, with the children sleeping until 07:30 hours. Needless to say the coach was late, the driver needed his statutory EU cigarette break and Jane finally tumbled into bed at half past one. She wasn't best pleased when Tom rang four hours later.

He continued to ring through much of Saturday. They were on the ferry, they were in France, he hated it, he loved it, could we put some more money on the mobile phone we'd lent him?

"I've already done it."

"Are you sure?"

"Tom, if you didn't spend so much time ringing us for more money on the phone, you wouldn't need more money on the phone." Tom didn't see the logic of this. There was already £25.00 worth of credits, and he was only away for five days – the omens for the teenage bills weren't looking good. Neither were our stress levels – suddenly he seemed too young to be away from us.

I was just settling down to the watch the football scores when the phone rang again. Jessica dived on it, anticipating a twenty minute gossip with her friend Lucy. I wrestled it off her and went in to the kitchen. Tom sounded upset. "What's the matter?"

"The coach has crashed," he said.

"What?"

Between the poor quality of the line and his own shock I could barely hear him. I caught the words "tyre" and "burst." Jane came running in and took over, reassuring him as best she could. He was alright – everyone was alright – but he was shaken and he was standing on the side of a road in France. "I want to drive straight over there," Jane said. So did I.

That's it isn't it? Once you've got children you're never without them. Jane and I had planned it all – Valentine's Day, Tom was in France, Jessica and Ben were going to be packed off to Granny's. We'd got *Calendar Girls* and a bottle of wine and at last, time for each other. And now we couldn't think straight for worrying about Tom.

He phoned again about eight o'clock that night.

They'd finally reached the hostel. He was loving it, but wasn't impressed with French food. They were off to Disney tomorrow and he was going to ask Sarah to go on Thunder Mountain with him.

"I think I love her, Dad," he said.

"Don't you think ten's a bit young for that?"

"No, I definitely love her – I want to buy her a present."

"What were you thinking of?"

"Something that looks expensive, but that doesn't cost a lot. Something that's really cheap…"

I recounted this to Jane as we finished the wine. "Hmmm," she said. "Now who does that remind me of?" So, no need for a paternity test after all…

Wishful Thinking

A friend of mine turned to me in despair last Monday. "I asked our two to wash up yesterday," she said. "They threatened to call Childline."

Washing up after Sunday lunch. That takes you back doesn't it? I'd struggle doggedly through Mum's rhubarb crumble, then stand next to my Dad, tea towel in hand, while he tossed soaking plate after soaking plate into the drainer. "Make sure they're properly dry," he chanted.

"Actually, Dad, new research shows that it's more hygienic to let them dry naturally."

"Give them a good wipe. Make sure they're dry," he would repeat, just in case I hadn't heard.

"No, Dad. They've done some research at a university. Tea towels are full of bacteria – you're just transferring the germs on to the plates."

"Once they're properly dry you can put them away," said the man who regularly complained that I never listened to what he was saying.

When we bought our house Jane suggested we have a dishwasher. In the years between leaving home and listening to Jane I'd had the single bloke's traditional attitude to washing up. Pile it up until there was nothing left that was clean, and then do it – if the takeaway was closed. Unscheduled washing up was only required if you got lucky with some girl. So all in all I couldn't really see the need to spend three hundred quid on a dishwasher.

I am now not afraid to admit that I was wrong – totally, utterly, wrong. Twelve years and three children later I'd rather divorce my wife than the dishwasher. As far as I'm concerned, it's right up there at the top of the inventions list – way ahead of minor trivialities like the wheel. What's more it will stay there until Mr. Zanussi's boffins come up with the Shoe-Cleaning-and-Polishing machine.

Another distant memory of my Dad. I'd stand at his side as he brushed shoes with something approaching religious fanaticism. I do it with my attention on a football commentary and the kids nowhere to be seen. But my biggest gripe is the time it takes.

Jessica ran in an inter-school cross country on Friday. I'm not sure why they held it in a field that had just been used for the World Ploughing Championship, but they did. She wrote off her trainers warming up, and had to race in her football boots. Tom chipped in with another pair of boots, plus there were three pairs of school shoes, my shoes and then came Jane. "Oh, hello, dear. Are you polishing shoes?"

No, my love, surrounding myself with half a field helps me to hear the football on the radio. (Tip to newly married men – you don't actually say that out loud.)

Anyway, by the time I'd scraped, wiped, scrubbed, put polish on, taken it off and opened another beer to see me through, it took from kick off to Man Utd's second goal. And then I had to finish off with 'Sports Gel.'

"Put this on them," Jane said, passing me a trendy grey tube. "It might help to keep the water out."

"What about the three tons of mud?" I muttered, and thought wistfully of dubbin.

So if the scientists are out there looking for somewhere to direct the appliance of science, may I suggest my children's footwear? And then when Tom gets married he can convince his wife the kitchen needs space for a Shoe-Clean-Machine.

"Absolutely crucial, darling," he'll say. "I can still hear my Dad moaning now. But we'll buy some brushes and polish for when he comes round, just to make the old boy feel welcome…"

Saint Karen

The first time Tom had a proper hair cut he was violently sick. A friend of ours – who did some hairdressing on the side – came round one evening. Tom sat on a chair in the kitchen, a towel was draped round him, and trimming commenced. Somehow Tom managed to swallow a stray curl. His reaction was instantaneous and spectacular. Carrots, banana and Ribena shot across the kitchen. Our friend left wearing one of Jane's spare tops and it took about a month to get rid of the smell. "Next time," said Jane, "You can take him to a proper hairdresser."

I put it off as long as I could, but eventually I found myself in town, a long haired Tom in tow. It was very early on Saturday morning – if he was going to throw up I didn't want anyone else to see it. At that time I had my hair cut in Newcastle and didn't really know the local shops. It turned out to be too early for most of them, but then I found one.

"Karen's," it said on the window, "Gents Hairdressing." I gingerly pushed the door open. To my intense relief it was empty. Karen was drinking a cup of coffee.

"Do you cut children's hair?" I asked nervously.

She seemed to have a kind face. "Sure," she said.

"Great. Come on, Tom." I should really have asked,

"Do you mind if my son is sick in your shop?" but I wasn't brave enough.

But Tom wasn't sick. He was fine – and at the end of it he looked vastly better than our friend had made him look.

We've been going to Karen's ever since. During that time she has tolerated Jessica playing hopscotch on her newly tiled floor, and cut Ben's hair kneeling down when he refused to climb into the chair. The woman is a saint – the trouble is, everyone else knows it now.

"What's this?" I said when Ben and I walked in on Saturday. "I've never seen you so busy."

"Mothers' Day," she said.

"Mothers' Day?" I repeated dimly. "What's that got to do with it?"

She gave me the patient look that had first convinced me she wouldn't mind if Tom was sick on her. "Next week," she said. "Men are going to see their mothers. They don't want nagging about their hair. It's the same at Christmas." Obvious when you think about it I suppose.

So Ben and I sat quietly and waited, and all around me I listened to people speaking a foreign language. For a while I'd felt vaguely uneasy saying, "Just tidy it up and cut the grey out." Now I realised that somehow I'd fallen asleep for several years and a whole new hairdressing language had come in while I dozed.

"Two at the sides and spiked at the front."

"Flat top for me please, and messy spikes for young Jason."

Men who didn't even need a haircut demanded, "Half at the sides, one on top," and came out more or less bald. Even people a lot older than me were speaking the language – blokes for whom the words 'just chop the grey out' would mean shaving the whole lot off. (I think that's a 'zero' in today's terms.)

I sat in the chair and asked Karen about it. "Tramlines," she said.

"Tramlines?"

"Patterns, letters…" she explained. "You can have those as well if you want. Shaved into your hair…"

For a few seconds I fantasised about going into work with the back of my head saying 'Pools.'

"Maybe not," I said, "Just tidy it up and cut the grey out…"

Lost in Cyberspace

Tom's best friend is Ollie – at least for this week. His mother rang me the other day. "Oliver was on the computer," she said. "Playing online – we couldn't get him off. It was dreadful. We said an hour. He ended up playing for two and a half. He had a screaming tantrum when we finally made him stop."

"Sounds familiar," I sighed. "What shall we do about it?"

Children – they're born and you count their fingers and toes, they wake you up in the night when they're teething, they start school and you worry about the teachers, they become teenagers and… No, I'm writing this at the weekend – I don't want to think about teenagers. And somewhere in the middle of all that ten year old boys discover online computer games – if you have a ten year old boy who hasn't done this yet, you may now wish to fall to your knees and give thanks.

It all started about a fortnight ago. Tom's computer game of the moment is *Halo*. Somehow I missed the fact that it's a 16. Jane didn't, and has been reminding me ever since. I'm not sure of the exact story, but it involves deep space, multiple aliens and wholesale carnage. It's difficult to establish contact with Tom when he's playing any computer game – with *Halo* it's impossible.

When I came downstairs last Monday he was already on the computer. I made the usual attempts at conversation, but without success. Eventually I wandered over to have a look. There was a mass free for all on *Halo*. I hadn't seen this scenario before. Some text suddenly appeared at the side of the screen:

"Iceman was killed by Happyboy."

"The Boss died."

I was still half asleep and it took me a while to realise that Tom was playing online. Then "Is that your best shot…" came up, followed by a seriously unpleasant American greeting. I dived for the off button – and Tom and I had a lengthy inquest.

This is where Ollie comes in. Because Tom wants to play online, and so does Ollie – and their pal, James. That is, Stinger, Deathray and Captain Blood want to play online. "Come on, Dad. I can't just be 'Tom'," he told me. "That's way uncool…"

I duly phoned their parents and now they play each other on Friday nights and Sunday mornings. I have this nagging feeling they should be outside kicking a ball about, but I suppose that's progress.

"How are you doing?" I asked Tom during the last game. I leaned over and touched F1 to bring the score up. It flickered briefly on the screen – he was leading, just. Then there was a shot and his body was flying through the air. "Dad," he screamed. "You stopped me seeing! Just get lost will you?"

What did Ollie's mother say? "Tantrum?" Never heard the word.

To be honest, Tom's got a fight on his hands. Ollie's only had the game ten days, but he's showing real promise. What's his mother worried about? His school report will be impressive. "Oliver has made excellent progress in online gaming this term. Maths and English do give some cause for concern but his destruction of the android mutants was especially impressive. A promising start – well done, Oliver!"

And what am I doing while the battles rage? I'm babysitting – to make sure their password protected game stays protected, on guard against the sleazier side of the internet. No doubt we'll find it, sooner or later.

Being a parent – it's like war isn't it? Eternal vigilance required...

Easter Parade

As a general rule I don't do sad things. At least I don't think so – Jane may well disagree. But every year on Good Friday I clear out the garage. Don't ask me how it started, but I do. And to tell you the truth, I've grown to like it. Winter ends, the clocks change, I clear out the garage, and summer can't be far away.

"Right, you three. Listen to me." (I always like to start with a little speech). "I'm now going to clear out the garage. In three hours it will be tidy. I expect it to be that way in September." Even as I'm saying it, I know that by May chaos will have returned and the door will once again be blocked by bikes, rakes, spades, assorted cricket stumps and the top of a sandpit we haven't used for two years.

Sadly, Jane now seems to be developing another bank holiday ritual – clearing out my wardrobe, (just to confirm that I've put on weight since last year). She hasn't been doing it for that long, but the Salvation Army no longer seem surprised by my Easter Saturday appearance. "Another year," the captain smiles. "Another hole on your belt."

This year their pile was larger than average, mainly thanks to Jessica. Standing in the bedroom trying on a succession of clothes, (many of which only just escaped the axe last year), I can usually convince Jane that with a bit of diet and exercise they'll fit again. My daughter's hysterical laughter, and her polite enquiry, "Is that meant to look as though it's going to burst?" made sure that the Sally Army wouldn't be entirely dependant on sales of *War Cry* this year.

But these two rituals, however much they've become traditional, are just warm-ups. The regular Easter event for us is the trip to Grandma's. Between you and me I can think of better ways of spending Easter Sunday than an hour and a half on the A1, but that's what families are for. There's an air of gloom as we get into the car. The kids don't fancy the journey, I don't fancy the traffic, and Jane fancies being single again.

But for some reason – and I've got my Dad to thank for this one as well – all this puts me in jolly-quizmaster mode. We'd happily wile away long trips in the Ford Anglia with family quizzes, and I'm determined my kids will have the same fun – whether they like it or not. "Right," I say before we've even reached the motorway, "Who wants a quiz?"

Jane groans, Tom turns up his Walkman or his Gameboy (quite possibly both), but the other two – bless them – will still humour me.

We always start with I-Spy. In previous years Ben was the absolute star at this. "Something beginning with H," he'd shout.

"Hedge?"

"No."

"House?"

"No."

"I know! Horse."

"No."

And we'd plod desperately on. "Hedgehog?" Had he seen that squashed one?

"No."

Eventually we had to give in.

"Tree!" Ben would yell triumphantly.

Now school has spoiled the fun – OK it's progress, but it's taken all the mystery out of the game. This Easter when he says, "Something beginning with F," we'll be depressingly sure that field, farm or fox will pretty soon follow.

Meanwhile, the noise from Tom's electronic equipment is getting steadily louder, as he tries to block out the reminders that he was once an uncool five year old. The boy should look on the bright side – only thirty years to go and he'll be spending Easter with the Salvation Army...

Bundles of Joy

"So how's Claire?"

"Yeah, she's good – excellent."

"How long now – five weeks? Six weeks?"

"We had the baby two months ago…"

"Two months!? Are you sure?"

Amazing isn't it? When your own wife is pregnant it lasts about two years, when it's someone else's wife it takes three months. I'd last spoken to David a few weeks ago – at least that's what I thought. It turned out to be closer to six months, and in that time his life had been irreversibly altered.

"Having a baby won't change our lives." How many times have you heard people say that? They're absolutely right. Their old life – the one with restaurants in it, and weekends away and quiet nights in – won't change. It will end. And here comes your new life – the one full of sterilisers and formula and (I'm sorry if you're having a meal) sick trickling down your back at four in the morning.

We'd had Tom home for about five days. It was the middle of the night, and I was walking up and down the bedroom trying to get him to sleep. "What have we done?" I said to Jane. "Where's the instruction book?"

"There isn't one," she said. "We're stuck."

Later on our exchanges became even more terse. We used to live in a house that overlooked the sea. The wind started in Russia, came across the North Sea and in at our bedroom window. It didn't put my wife in the best of moods when she ws breast-feeding at three in the morning. Eventually we introduced a rule that nothing we said to each other between midnight and breakfast counted.

"And I'm tired…" David was saying. "In fact, I'm not tired, I'm exhausted." It's not until you become a parent that you understand why Amnesty International get so worked up about sleep deprivation. Or why the KGB always came to call just before dawn. I remember going to work a few weeks after Tom was born. There were a lot of things on my desk marked urgent. Some were probably very urgent. I couldn't have cared less. All I wanted to do was push them on the floor, lie down on the desk and go to sleep.

"And all my free time has gone," he wailed. Free time? I looked it up in a text book. Apparently it's what you had before the children arrived. I can't remember that far back. David and his wife struck me as the sort of couple who would have another child. I thought it might be kind of me to give him an idea of what life would be like.

"What are you planning to do on Saturday?" I asked.

"I thought I might go to football," he said. "Pools are playing Notts County – another step towards Cardiff."

"Don't bother," I said. "Drive to Brownies instead. And then drive to martial arts. Dash home, eat half a sandwich, check the score on text if you're lucky and then drive back to Brownies. And then look up the date of the play-off final – try and book your mother-in-law."

"Anyway," I said. "Apart from all that, how's the baby?"

"Oh God," he said, "She's just perfect, she's got these tiny little fingers and…"

I let him carry on for five minutes. I didn't tell him that one day she'll be sitting in the bath and will look up at him with those beautiful blue eyes. "Daddy," she'll say.

"Yes, darling?"

"I've done a poo, Daddy."

And David will have to put his hand in and fish it out. After all, there's only so much other people can tell you. Some things are best discovered for yourself…

Identity Crisis

My passport ran out a couple of months ago – a shame, as I was one of the few people in the world that liked their own passport photo. Already six years out of date when it went into service, the photo showed me in my late twenties when I'm really – well, a bit older than that. Frankly I thought it was still a pretty good likeness, although it did take me a while to get past Spanish immigration last summer. "So what do you think?" I said to Tom. "That still looks like me doesn't it? Should be OK to use again."

"Well…" Tom replied, making the first attempt of his life at being tactful. "Your hair's not quite the same colour, and your forehead's got more lines on it and…"

"Don't go on," I said, "I already know I've got children."

With some glee, Jane walked in and twisted the knife. "Oh look, Tom," she said, "I used to have a boyfriend that looked like that. I expect he's older and fatter now."

"He'll look like that for another ten years," I said, "I've got a couple of these photos left somewhere."

"No good," she said. "It's got to look like you – not like how you want to look."

I took some convincing, but eventually I found myself spinning the seat round in one of those little booths, dreading the inevitable result. But technology had moved on and now I was very politely asked if the first photo was OK. It wasn't Johnny Depp, but it didn't look too bad so I pressed the button. The machine must have lied to me – what came out didn't look anything like the preview, or much like me come to that. But I was too mean to pay another three quid so it would have to do.

"You'll need that certifying," Jane said when I got home.

"No, I won't," I replied. "Look – section ten. That's only if your appearance has changed considerably from the last photo. Mine hasn't." Jane muttered something I didn't catch.

I'd left it late to renew the passport so I went into the Post Office to use their express service. The woman behind the counter looked doubtfully at the two photos. "Is that you, dear? You'll need this new one certifying."

"No I won't," I said. "It's me…"

She was still doubtful, but then the other two girls working there got involved.

"It is him, Jean."

"Yeah, it is, Jean. Definitely – he's just older and fatter." Thanks – but at least I'd won a majority verdict.

Jessica came up to me a couple of days later. "Dad," she said, in the tone of voice that meant I wasn't going to like what came next. "You know your passport photo…"

"What about it?"

"Well you weren't really telling the truth were you?"

"How do you mean?" I asked, but I knew I was skewered. "Telling the Truth" is a big thing in our house. The rule is more or less that anything you've done is OK, providing you tell the truth about it. If we can get the children to do that now, Jane and I think we might have a chance when they're teenagers.

"Because…" Jessica went on, "You wanting to use that old photo, that was sort of telling a lie wasn't it?"

I stammered something pathetic about different sorts of lies. I tried to tell her that some days I just didn't fancy crashing through middle age at ever increasing speeds.

She looked at me with her big brown eyes. "But you're my Daddy," she said. "And I love you – even if you are fatter."

And if that doesn't make it a price worth paying, nothing does…

Ready, Steady, Mess

There are two pools of milk on the worktop. An empty Weetabix packet lies on its side. A wet spoon is lurking in the sugar and the floor is suddenly...crunchy. Looks like Tom's been getting his own breakfast again.

We are not a perfect family in the morning. The children do not skip happily down to breakfast, where the table is already set with a variety of cereals and fresh fruit. Tom gets up hideously early and then has to be dragged from the computer. Ben eats Sugar Puffs in front of a cartoon, and Jessica – assuming we can winkle her out of bed – very rarely eats breakfast at all. Occasionally though, Tom has been awake for so long that he's hungry by six-thirty. That's when I'll come down to find the kitchen looking like the "before" part of a TV makeover.

But at least he has a go. As a teenager I only tried cooking once. The expression on my Dad's face was enough, and that was it until I went away to college. I arrived at the learned academy that would transform me into a deep thinking intellectual at two-thirty on a September afternoon. Sometime around five my new roommate and I looked at each other and realised we were hungry – and that suddenly it was down to us. Rob turned to me and said, "Er...do you know how to boil an egg?"

The next morning he went to the bookshop and bought a cookbook. For the rest of that year we worked methodically through it – which was fine except we spent the first term living on starters, the second term on main courses and ate nothing but puddings from April to July.

So I'm determined that the kids will leave home capable of rather more than pressing the one minute button on the microwave – and I don't just mean knowing when to take the film off and when to stab holes in it. Tom's current speciality is bacon and eggs – I'm not sure that the house insurance covers the potent mixture of my son and hot fat but we live in hope. Obviously he makes a bit of a mess, but I'm afraid that's genetic. Have I cooked a meal? Has every knife been used? Is every surface covered in meat sauce? Guilty as charged.

But the question is, once they've cooked it, will they eat it? Tom and Jessica are not adventurous eaters, and I lay the blame for this squarely at the door of small jars of baby food. When Jane was pregnant with Jessica I was in charge of the weekly trudge round Tesco. I usually bought about ten of those little jars. Carrot and Banana? Apricot and Chicken? To be honest I could never tell the difference between them – they all tasted of cardboard. By the time Ben arrived we couldn't be bothered any more, so whatever we ate, we simply mashed it up for Ben. Stew and dumplings? No problem – it looks a bit brown, but then what doesn't when it's been in the blender? I think I put bacon, egg, sausage and beans in there one time. Whatever it was, Ben ate it happily.

And the net result of this? While Tom runs a mile from anything different, and Jessica would happily live on cheese sandwiches and chocolate, Ben eats it all.

"Is it spicy, Dad?"

"Yeah, a bit…"

"Great," and in goes his fork. Italian, Chinese, Indian – it doesn't matter. OK he stops short of a vindaloo, but it's only a matter of time. There's only one worry – he will insist on drinking my beer with it…

Split Personalities

"Jessica, what did you just do?"

Silence. "Jessica, tell me what you did to Ben." I know what she did but I want her to confess.

Silence. "Jessica, for the last time. Did I just see you stamp on your little brother?"

"Maybe."

"There's no maybe about it, go up to your bedroom and you can stay there for the rest of the day."

"He deserved it."

And you probably know how it develops from there…

But then we come to her school report. "Jessica is a delight to teach. She is always ready to help others in the class and has made a positive contribution throughout the year, although she is perhaps a little quiet at times. I shall miss teaching her and wish her well for the future."

Honestly, that's what it said – "a little quiet." I still can't believe it.

So which is the real Jessica? I have lived a few years now, I've met a lot of people, but I've never seen anyone lose their temper like Jessica. And yet her reports are bursting with comments like that. As far as I can tell she's never been in trouble since the day she crossed the threshold of the reception class.

The boys on the other hand are much simpler – by and large what you see is what you get, and I suspect that how they behave at home is how they are at school. Is that just my children – or does it mean that women are deeper, more complex creatures than us simple men? (It's alright, I already know the answer – Jane told me.) But even the boys have their moments, and there are days when I think my role as a parent is to get more and more confused.

When Tom was born we had a lot of nice text book theories about how we'd raise the children – our boys would be put in touch with their feminine side, the girls would be encouraged to play with cars and grow up to be tank commanders. Gradually we've shredded them all. I can still remember the day Tom first bit his toast into the shape of a gun and shot his Mother in the back.

And here comes another teaser for the text books, because Jane's away on a course this week so I'm a one parent family for a few days. As soon as we've waved her off at the station the characters of the children will change. Jessica will promptly mature by about ten years – she'll no longer have to be wrestled from her bed in the morning and will come downstairs ready for school, hair brushed and face shining. For the next few days she'll be helpful beyond belief. Tom on the other hand will go the other way – every time Jane's away his behaviour slides downhill, because he knows that's a sure way to get my attention. So maybe the text books were right after all. What do they say – don't reward bad behaviour with attention? I haven't a clue, and they're not even teenagers yet…

But enough of this self-analysis and back to Jane's course. How on earth it has been arranged to clash with play-off week I do not know, but it has. To be honest I think the children are getting a bit stale at school. Wouldn't a few days holiday benefit them while she's away – broaden their minds, see new places, expand their horizons and all that? I'm sure school would understand. After all I'd promise it was somewhere educational – somewhere like, say, Bristol...

The Famous Four

Let us start with a small prayer of thanks – Jane is back from her course, and life is normal again. That is, the kids are still rioting, but mercifully I'm now only responsible 50% of the time. Single parent family? I wouldn't last a week.

Not that Jane didn't give me instructions before she went – the list was pinned to the fridge. It was quite detailed – well, it ran to three pages if you want the truth. We sent twenty thousand troops to Iraq with less information.

While Jane was away I thought I'd have a go at being an old fashioned Dad. Plenty of fresh air and exercise and 'just say no' to the computer. I stopped short of suggesting we camp in the garden, but only because we don't have a tent. I'm not sure what brought this on, but I have the vague feeling that I should stop reading *Famous Five* books to Jessica.

Enid Blyton can be a dangerous woman. Tom's having a tantrum and won't come off the computer? No problem. Come bedtime you just open up *Five go to Billycock Hill* and your parenting troubles are over. Suddenly you're in a different world.

Children voluntarily go and play in the garden. They build dams and throw sticks into streams. They swim in the sea (Enid clearly never went in the sea off Hartlepool – *Five get Hypothermia* doesn't have quite the same ring). They say things like, 'Golly, thanks, Father,' and then they drink ginger beer and tell you that it tastes 'wizard.'

Neither do Julian, Dick, Ann and George say 'I'm bored,' (and *they* don't have a thousand quid's worth of electronic equipment), and they never, ever – eight year old daughters please note – turn to their father and say "Hello?" in the tone of voice that suggests you are a parent of very little brain.

Sadly I'd have to keep my part of the bargain, which might mean building a tree house instead of checking the football scores on teletext. Maybe Ikea could do one in a pack?

Anyway, Jane was away, the sun was shining and I was not going to spend the day listening to Tom and his mate Ollie blasting aliens. "Come on you four," I said. "We're off to the woods."

"But we're at level six…" Tom protested

"Save it," I said. "We're going to have an adventure."

We went to the shop for supplies – no ginger beer but plenty of Mars Bars – and half an hour later we were in the woods, standing at the bottom of a seriously steep hill. "To the summit," I commanded, "Or no chocolate."

Jessica led the charge. They soon slowed to a more sensible pace, but they made it. Hanging on to trees, pulling each other up, working together they reached the top. And then all we had to do was go back down…

"Can we go on that track over there?" Tom asked.

"Not a chance – there's a stream by it. There'll be loads of mud…"

"But it's the most difficult way – it's a challenge."

What could I say? Enid would have been proud of them. "Just try and keep out of the mud then." They didn't of course, but Tom's trainers should be serviceable again if they go through the washing machine another six or seven times.

They were exhausted when I put them to bed that night. Just before he fell asleep Tom said, "That was a brilliant day, Dad. Can we do it again?"

That was all I wanted to hear. Old fashioned Dad, one – computer games, nil. Absolutely spiffing…

Stress Factor 10

I've had enough – the children have been beating me with their favourite sticks again. Tom and Jessica have both had a go – the sticks are labelled 'David's parents' and 'Emma's lounge.'

David is an only child. He is also Tom's new best friend. What David's parents won't do for him is nobody's business. As far as I can tell they are prepared to live entirely on worms so they can buy the wretched child a Porsche for his seventeenth birthday and fuel him with chocolate along the way. Spoilt? You can't imagine it...

They also have a depressingly liberal attitude to the videos David watches. What do we do – send Tom round with a list of what he can and can't watch? Well, the banned list could include the last five minutes of England versus France for a start. All you can do is trust the judgement of the other parents, but at David's house the boundaries are a lot further away than they are at home. So Tom and I now have a monotonously regular conversation.

"Can I watch *Matrix*, Dad?"

"I don't think so, Tom. Not just yet."

"David's seen all three of them."

"Well, that's up to David's parents."

"I'm the only one in my class that hasn't seen it – everyone's laughing at me."

I know for a fact that there's a vicar's son in Tom's class – if he's even seen the more challenging episodes of *Postman Pat* I'll be amazed.

Jessica meanwhile is now friends with The Richest Girl in the Class. Emma, apparently, has her own lounge attached to her bedroom – which is, of course, stuffed with TVs, videos, PS2's, iPods and every other must-have electrical device. As far as I can tell she's already on Amex's mailing list. The fact that Emma's parents are so busy working that they don't seem to have seen their daughter since Easter is lost on Jessica.

We've therefore spent a large part of the last week saying "no" to our eldest two. No, you can't see *Troy*. No, you can't have an iPod, and no, we are not moving to a house we can't afford. This has not gone down well.

I've been trying to write this column for ninety minutes. During that time we've had three fights, two tantrums and a packet of Haribos sprayed all over the kitchen floor. Now they've all been sent to their bedrooms – so Jessica's decided to practise her recorder. I can hear it through the wall. I love my daughter very much, but right this minute I know precisely what I want to do with her recorder.

I went to the doctors the other day. He said my blood pressure was up. Well, there's a surprise – then again he should have taken it after Steven Gerrard's back pass.

"Are you getting enough exercise?" he asked.

"Well, I often carry a hysterical child upstairs and throw it into a bedroom."

"Do you set aside regular time each day for relaxation?"

"Yes – absolutely."

"Excellent," he beamed. "And when's that?"

"Immediately after I've drunk two bottles of lager."

That may not have been the answer he was looking for, but what do you do? You can't bring the children up in splendid isolation but there are times when it's seriously tempting. Do you simply throw TVs, videos and if you can afford it, enough money at your kids? Or do you give them that infinitely more valuable commodity – time? The answer's obvious, and we've some real quality family time to look forward to this week. It's on Thursday night, at 5 o'clock – back passes and blood pressure permitting...

Mister Consistent

Ben lost his temper and threw a cricket stump at me the other day. It missed, but only just. Was it deliberate? I don't know – at the time I didn't care. I was tired from work, the sun was shining, and I'd drunk two glasses of red wine.

Then Jessica bumped into me yesterday. I'd just told her off so it may have been deliberate – I don't know. But it made me spill my tea – so I lost my temper, sent her upstairs and came pretty close to smacking her. After all, I was tired from work, the sun wasn't shining and I hadn't drunk any red wine.

"Be consistent," the parenting books tell you. "Children appreciate boundaries. Good parents let children know how far they can go – and no further. Make rules and stick to them – consistently." That's what the experts say, and as a parent of nearly eleven years standing I say... Well, they can't print what I say.

Because consistency is impossible. Sometimes you're tired, sometimes you're not. Sometimes you're happy, sometimes you're sad. Sometimes you'll dash the length of the garden to stop them attacking each other...and sometimes they can just sort it out themselves – after all, it doesn't take that long to drive to A&E.

Do you do that – enforce boundaries? Set rules and stick to them? Be 100% consistent all the time? If the answer is "yes" may I politely suggest words along the lines of "Get a life?"

Take last week, for example. Did we religiously enforce bedtime? You must be joking. I considered it a vital part of my children's education to watch the penalty shoot-out. If you're going to let them stay up to see in Year 2000, then Beck's impersonation of Jonny Wilkinson has to be on the list as well. Besides, the sooner the children learn that the main function of football is to make you suffer the happier they'll be. I have to get them ready for a lifetime supporting 'Pools.

So Mister Consistent I'm not. Jane and I talk about it from time to time. The conversation is pretty well rehearsed now.

"We've got to do something about Tom/Jessica/Ben." (Whichever one is the problem this week.)

"We have to be more consistent."

"I know…"

"I'm not criticising you but…"

"OK, OK, we'll start at the weekend. When we've both got some energy back…"

Except that it never happens at the weekend, and on Monday you've still the same nagging doubt that you're not doing it quite right. And those wretched *Famous Five* books I'm still reading to Jessica keep reminding me of a golden age of perfectly disciplined children. The trouble is, the reality was very different.

My Dad used to tell me a story about a pound of apples (I think that's about four hundred grams these days). He'd been sent to the shop for the apples. He was a child, he was hungry, so he ate one on the way home. When he got home his father weighed the apples – then he took his belt to my Dad.

Would I have been hit for that? If my Mother had been baking and she'd needed exactly a pound I might have been sent back to the shop, but hit? Never.

And what would happen today – well apart from the fact that Jane hasn't time to bake and apples now grow in little plastic bags of four or six, we'd have a major celebration. "You've eaten some fruit, Jessica! Brilliant." We'd congratulate ourselves on an amazing new parenting strategy – and then we'd probably give her a Mars Bar as a reward. But at least we'd manage to do that consistently...

Seeing Red

Well, thank goodness it's over. Greece have won, Sven's tactics – if you find out what they were, let me know – are a fading memory, and our house will shortly return to normal.

This isn't a recognised medical condition, but Euro 2004's just like the World Cup – it sends me mad. I develop a sudden obsession with wall charts. Given that every publication this side of *Pigeon Fanciers World* gives you a cut-out-and-keep guide to the festivities, I'm not short of raw material. The children can't open the fridge without seeing England's route to the final (whatever happened to that?) and I've got the England squad on the bathroom wall. Tom's a big fan of Wayne Rooney, but I think he draws the line at going to the toilet with him.

The children are used to their Dad going mad – the really bad news for them is that the condition affects Jane as well. Her interest in football on a day to day basis is somewhere below zero. Then every two years she suddenly becomes an instant expert, and refuses to budge from the settee for the duration of the tournament. She's still receiving counselling for Zidane's two last minute goals, but it's the pundits that really get to her.

Gary Lineker says something mildly controversial

and Jane hurls a cushion at the TV. "We're defending too deep, you idiot," she yells. "We need someone in the hole." Tom suggested his sister should be put in a hole and received a straight red – thirty minutes in the bedroom sin bin.

We're off to Spain soon so suddenly she's a language coach as well. We were watching them the other night and Lawro started talking about Baraja. Jane was not impressed with the pronunciation. "Barracker?" she sneered. "Barracker? It's Bar – aha." She made a noise like she was clearing her throat and then sat there repeating it to herself. Tom and I thought we were watching the game with Donald Duck.

But at least the teams came out of the tunnel wearing all their kit – I wish I could say the same for my son. If Ronaldo gets a yellow card for whipping his shirt off then Tom must start every game dangerously close to an early bath.

I collected him from school last week. He was playing cricket and there wasn't much time.

"Are you sure you've got everything, Tom?"

"Yes."

"Cricket stuff?"

"Uh-huh."

"Homework? Anything else you need?"

"No."

"I don't mind waiting if you want to have a really good think…"

"No."

I breathed a sigh of relief and off we went. Two minutes before the game was due to start he came out of the dressing room.

"Dad?"

"What?"

"I've left my trainers at school."

It was too late to go back so he had to play in his school shoes. What is it about boys? You could wallpaper our house with notes from school. "Tom has lost…" "Brendan's shirt has gone missing," "If anyone has seen Neil's trousers…" Not for the life of me can I ever remember one of those notes featuring a girl's name.

So that's the big advantage of being a professional footballer. Not the money, not the fame – it's the kit man. Ronaldo's twinkling feet wouldn't look half so impressive if he was wearing his school shoes. No more lost boots two minutes before kick off – it must be like having your Mum follow you round the world. Which, of course, rules Tom out of all the major tournaments. Jane's unavoidably detained at home – she's on the settee, hurling abuse at Gary Lineker…

How To Shop

I've finished telling lies – that is, I've written all the holiday postcards. "Jane's reading, sun's shining, children in pool and I'm drinking beer." For some reason I can't write that – I have to write something suitable for each person.

So Gran was told, "Weather good, children all fine." Our friends' postcards were along the lines of "Hot, don't want to come back, gin cheap but tastes like petrol," and for some reason the little old lady next door received, "We are visiting a cheese factory tomorrow." A cheese factory? Tom is more likely to renounce electronic entertainment – but Joan could relate to that.

To be fair, I could have shocked everyone and written, "Children behaving themselves." Tom especially – we've hardly had a peep out of him. That's because he's brought his Game Boy.

"Where's Tom? Let me guess, in his bedroom." Here we are in Spain and he's developed an aversion to sunlight that Dracula would envy, and keeps talking about someone called Rayquaza. This is apparently a Pokemon he's trying to catch – alternatively he could have inside information on Chelsea's latest signing.

He's even playing happily with Jessica – thanks to us discovering a link cable so their Game Boys can talk to each other. Without doubt, that was my greatest ever piece of shopping.

"We need a link cable, Dad."

"Why's that, Tom?"

"So Jessica and I can play against each other."

I can see the advantages to that – more peace and quiet with my beer for one – but I'm compelled to point out the realities. "Tom, we are in a small town in Spain. The chance of you finding a link cable is somewhere below zero."

Tom won't accept this and eventually the combination of needing to buy food and his ceaseless nagging drive us into town. We go into electrical shop after electrical shop. There seems to be a phenomenal demand for radios in this town, but Game Boys? We might as well be looking for Elvis.

"Dad, Dad, look!" Tom shrieks in excitement and points down an alley at a shop. It's called *@ccesories*. I'm astonished – there might be a chance after all, and we start running – just in case every other English family needs a link cable. Sadly when we get there we find it does indeed sell accessories – as defined by a fourteen year old girl who's short of jewellery. Tom is downcast. Traipsing round town in eighty degree heat is not my idea of fun, but there'll be no peace unless we explore every possibility. "Come on," I say, and drag him into one more shop. Quite clearly it only sells Flamenco CDs, but it's our last hope.

I've long ago abandoned my attempts to speak Spanish. "You sell Game Boy?" I ask hopefully.

The shopkeeper sighs as though he's been asked this a hundred times. "Go out," he says. "Three left, two right."

And there it is. *Sunshine*, it's called. I'm so happy I go back to speaking Spanish.

"Habla Inglesi?" I ask.

"Non," the girl replies. My heart sinks. How do I explain what I need?

"Game Boy Advance?" I ask pathetically.

Her face lights up in a smile. Brilliant – she only knows three words of English and they're 'Game Boy Advance.' We are led over to a small display and there, nestling in a corner, is the only link cable this side of Valencia. Tom is ecstatic, and peace and quiet breaks out all round.

And so we're due to come home tomorrow. Jane's busy packing and the kids are desperately checking to see how much spending money I've got left. Not much is the answer. I've been down to the supermarket and stocked up on Spanish sausage – the ones you hang in the kitchen and carve pieces off for months to come. To be honest, I wasn't sure you could bring food back into the country.

"I think you can," Jane said. "But you're not allowed to give it to pigs in case you start another foot and mouth epidemic."

"But I can eat it?"

"No problem," she said. "The Government knows what it's doing..."

Thanks, Dad

Jessica shook me awake. "I've been sick, Daddy," she said.

"Where?"

"In the bath."

I looked at the clock. 3:58. "Happy birthday, darling," I said, and crawled off to clean it up.

As a general rule we try and encourage our children to aim at the toilet when they're ill. Clearly Jessica had needed a larger target. I looked down: pasta and cheese in a light chocolate sauce. Disgusting. I spooned it out with one of Ben's plastic boats that was obviously designed for the purpose – and then I tried to find somewhere to sleep.

Jessica had moved into Ben's room for one night – with Becky and Rachel, a double sleepover in honour of her birthday. Now she'd fallen asleep next to Jane, but clearly I couldn't let the Jessica's friends go home and say they'd woken up with her Dad – besides, I wouldn't fit into the sleeping bag. Ben was in Jessica's room. I sighed and trudged down to the sofa – at least if I couldn't sleep I could watch the underwater truck racing, or whatever top quality sport was on at four in the morning.

That was a few days ago. I seem to have lost the ability to sleep ever since – a bit worrying when there are still nine months of the football season to go.

So apart from the new striker your team needs, what else do you think about when you're awake in the middle of the night? This week my thoughts have turned to gratitude, or the lack of it.

To put it mildly, Tom was quite unpleasant while Jessica was opening her birthday presents. "Ten quid," he said when she opened the first one. "Thirteen ninety-nine," greeted a Busted CD.

Becky and Rachel looked on in amazement. Neither of them had an older brother, so how could we explain? "Tom," we hissed, "Will you please be quiet?"

"About a fiver," he replied, as Jessica unwrapped some junior make up.

Then he went into adding machine mode – a clear message that we'd spent more on Jessica than him and that he'd be keeping a careful note come October. Another visit from the 'It's Not Fair' monster.

It turned up again yesterday. Off we trooped to see *Shrek2* – another instalment in the ongoing birthday celebrations, which (with a good deal of help from Jessica) seem to grow longer every year. Tickets for the cinema, popcorn, drinks, more profits for Mr. Haribo – the usual story. And what did my children say when they came out?

"Can we have an ice-cream?"

"That wasn't fair, Ben had two cartons of popcorn."

"You had more sweets than me."

"Well you had a bigger drink."

"Did not."

…And on and on until we got back to the car, and then they had a fight.

We once had a blissful Christmas Day with Ben. He opened every present carefully, examined it, played with it for a while and then beamed at us. "Just what I wanted," he said – while his brother and sister ripped away in a blizzard of wrapping paper. They paused occasionally, but only to check on whose stack was highest.

OK, I know they're not going to say, "Dad, we really appreciated that," or "On balance we think we've eaten enough sweets, Dad, especially as Jessica made herself sick the other night." But occasionally – just once – a simple "Thanks, Dad," would go down very nicely.

I suppose this begs the question of what sort of child I was. "You know," an Auntie said to me when I was about Tom's age, "You were perfectly obnoxious when you were younger." I didn't know what the word meant, but it was obviously a compliment. I shot straight off to my brand new dictionary to check. I never did like that Auntie...

Creative Accounting

We've spent a large chunk of the school holidays encouraging our children to tell lies – mainly because there are three of them. Where are we going this weekend? Swimming pool? Museum? It doesn't matter – wherever we go I'll be doing some complicated maths to make sure we get in as cheaply as possible. And part of that will mean being a little economical with the truth.

Two adults plus two children equals no problem. The all-purpose family ticket will always do the job. But have the extra bottle of red wine that leads to baby number three and there's trouble ahead. And when they reach the ages our children currently are – ten, nine and five – then the complications really begin.

'Children under five free.' I particularly like that one, especially if we're arriving in the car.

"Just wriggle down in your seat, Ben. If the man asks tell him you're four."

"But I'm five, Daddy. And soon I'm going to be six."

"I know you are, but just go back to being four will you?"

"Why?"

"Because then it's cheaper for us to get in and…" (here I resort to my most persuasive argument), "Dad will have more money to spend on sweets."

Ben is usually fine with this – the trouble comes when Tom or Jessica decide to go all moral on me. This is depressingly frequent.

"Isn't that telling a lie, Dad?"

"What is?"

"Saying Ben's four. That's not setting a very good example, Dad."

"It's only a small lie. Besides, the extremely-large-leisure-company that runs this isn't going to miss Ben's two quid."

"But you always say it's wrong to tell lies…"

And so I do. The basic message that we bring our children up by is "Tell us what's gone wrong and we'll sort it out. Just don't lie to us." The theory is that when they're teenagers this will change to, "Whatever you've done, whatever you want to do, we'll sit down and talk about it. Just don't lie to us." I'll let you know how it works out…

And for Tom being a teenager is not very far away – twenty six months and counting. Which means that when our car pulls up at the pay station I'll have a whole new set of problems with my hormonal son.

"Tom, don't forget you're twelve if they ask you."

"Don't you think it's time you stopped being such a cheapskate, Dad? You should have gone to the cashpoint like I said."

"Just do me this favour will you, Tom?"

"Might. Might not."

"Tom, it saves five quid if you're a child."

"So what's in it for me? Three quid and I'll be

twelve."

"One."

"Two pounds fifty."

And in the true tradition of family life, eventually we'll reach a compromise – probably around two forty-nine. Of course, Tom's already a teenager when it suits him – when he wants a PC game with a large "16" on the box, or when he wants to see a film that hasn't passed my wife's board of censors. At least Jane doesn't have all these confusing certificates – she issues a simple "yes" or "no."

We've seen all the main films with the children – *Lord of the Rings, Harry Potter* and so on. I think one was a PG and one was a 12A, but what's the difference? Can the children go to a PG on their own if we've talked to them first? Am I supposed to hold Ben's hand during a 12A? I haven't a clue.

Of course, we could always appoint Tom as film censor – and settle down to watch *Matrix Reloaded* for the next seven nights. Funny how he enjoyed *Brother Bear* so much...

Yikes

Right now he's trying to chew through my computer cable. A few minutes ago I caught him eating my cornflakes.

Before you think one of the boys has eaten too many E numbers I'll confirm the obvious – we've got a new kitten. He's called Yikes.

The name was Ben's choice, but being a democratic family we naturally put it to the vote. We had a short list of Tiger, Toby, Yo-Yo (a moment of inspiration from Jessica), Stripes, Weasley and Yikes.

My fiendishly clever voting system – designed to get the result you always wanted and available to the Government for a substantial fee – eventually whittled it down to Weasley and Yikes. On the grounds that he was ginger Jane had decided that Weasley was a fine name for a cat. This may have had something to do with her just finishing a Harry Potter – it can't have had anything to do with standing in the garden yelling "Weasie" at the top of your voice. Besides, Ben's threat of a major tantrum if we didn't choose Yikes was always going to be decisive.

When Jane and I first met we had three cats between us. Eventually two cases of old age and one encounter with a criminally aggressive Labrador saw them off. Secretly I quite enjoyed the interval where there was no litter tray to clean out, but I knew it couldn't last. Gradually the pressure for a new pet mounted. A puppy was the early favourite.

"We could take it for walks and love it, Dad."

"And play with it in the garden."

"So who's going to take it for a walk in the winter when it's cold and wet?"

"That could be your job, Dad."

No matter how much they begged, the practicalities meant no puppy. But it was impossible to resist the tidal wave of support for a kitten. Once Jessica's pal Freddie announced that his cat was pregnant there was no turning back, and I came home one day to a note. "Gone to look at kittens. J, T, J & B x."

"I love him," Jessica declared simply on their return. "And he loves me." After that we seemed to do even more shopping than we did before Tom was born. Two new feeding bowls arrived: a new place mat: a new bed: one of those hammocks you clip on to a radiator which the cat's supposed to sleep in and never does.

Eventually the great day arrived. Jessica carried him triumphantly over the threshold. She finally put him down about two days later, once he'd given her a quick nip.

I have – sorry, had – a pair of battered old beach shoes which I wore around the house. Not very elegant, but they were almost certainly the most comfortable pair of shoes anyone has ever owned. Foolishly, I left them near the kitten. He sniffed at them, put his paw in one of them, his head in the other and fell asleep. When he woke up he sniffed them again, and then used them to show us that he wasn't fully house trained. We should have stuck with Weasley after all.

Since then of course, I've grown to love him. To think that I ever suggested a name as stupid as Stripes. 'Yikes' fits him like a glove.

He's sitting on the table as I'm writing, watching the cursor flying across the screen. If the screen saver comes on he tries to catch it. You know, now I think back, I'm pretty sure it was my idea to get a kitten in the first place...

Creepy Crawlies

I was invited to play golf the other day – a rare event, but given my swing not entirely surprising. I checked the weather forecast. A temporary gap in the mid-summer monsoon season seemed a good chance to dig out my shorts. We teed off hideously early in the morning. The course was dotted with pools of stagnant water, breeding grounds for vampire mosquitoes. They must have seen me coming. "Wake up, lads, breakfast is heading up the fifth fairway. Look at those fat legs, it's a full English."

I've been dabbing the cream on ever since, but if I thought that was the end of my problems with God's smaller creatures, I was wrong.

Tom occasionally entertained himself on our Spanish holiday by nuking ants. He sat by the pool, filled his water pistol, and blasted away at the never ending column as they marched remorselessly towards the dustbin and yesterday's leftovers.

I must have had too much beer one day because I decided to conduct an experiment and dropped some of Jessica's chocolate on the floor. The ants came, inspected it and went away again, totally disinterested. Then they swarmed all over a piece of discarded banana. "Look at that," I said to the children. "They know more about tooth decay than we do. Worker ants, soldier ants, but no dentist ants."

"No San Miguel ants either," muttered my wife. I let it pass.

Having spent a large part of the holiday contemplating the behaviour of ants, I came home and completely forgot about them – until we found them in Jane's car.

"They're living in the back," Jane told me on Friday.

I added "De-ant J's car" to my weekend list, and made a mental note not to drive her car in shorts.

Over dinner we remembered that we'd left the cases on the drive while we waited for a lift to the airport. We'd obviously blocked the ants direct route to the previous night's pizza. They must have climbed on the cases, survived the baggage handlers and then decided the back of Jane's car was their new home.

"They're living on the crumbs the children drop," Jane said. If that's the case they'll be the fattest ants on the planet before very long.

I did my best with the vacuum cleaner. "There you are," I said confidently. "Job done."

Some hope – the children were in bed, football was on TV and there was a beer in my hand. Then Jane's car alarm went off. I zapped it and went back to the football. It went off again – and again. In the end we gave up and left the car unlocked overnight.

"You don't suppose there could be an ant in the alarm sensor, do you?" Jane said as we climbed into bed.

"Don't be ridiculous," I replied. A quick clean was one thing, dismantling the alarm system was quite another.

In the morning I drove the car round the block. "That'll sort it," I said to myself as I locked it. The alarm went off five minutes later. In desperation we called a man out.

His initial inspection pronounced the alarm system to be in perfect working order – except it wasn't. Jane explained our theory. Spanish ants in the alarm didn't seem to have been part of his mechanics' training course.

We were just contemplating major expense when Jane read the manual properly. "Turn the key twice to disable the alarm system." So that's what we did. Now we're waiting for the ants living in the sensor to die of old age. It's either that or sell the car – so just be careful if you see our ad in the 'For Sale' section…

Car Boot Capers

It started as a routine tidying of Ben's bedroom – one more attempt to discover the carpet under the sea of toys. Then something in Jane snapped. "Blow it," she said, or words to that effect. "We're going to do a car boot sale."

"I've asked around," I said two days later. "I've found the best one to go to. There's some bad news though."

"What's that?"

I tried to break it gently. My wife does not officially recognise any time before nine o'clock on a Sunday morning. "We need to be there at seven-thirty."

"Blow it," Jane said again.

The pile of toys, clothes and books now deemed surplus to requirements grew at a frightening speed. Jane's car was full in no time. Once we'd crammed the surplus into mine there was room for me and one child – a problem as I had to take two. I could drive – just – providing I didn't mind doing it with Old MacDonald's Farm jammed under my legs. Every time I changed gear a sheep said "baa."

"Are you sure you know where it is?" Jane asked on Sunday morning.

"Of course I do," I said. "It's on the left, off that big roundabout."

It was ominously quiet when we arrived. Being there first was one thing, being there before the organisers was quite another. I peered over the gate into a deserted field. A solitary cow stared back at me. There was no sign of a car boot sale. I glanced at Jane. She seemed to be writing something in her 'Reasons for Divorce' notebook.

At that moment a car went past with a microwave strapped to the roof. "Follow them," I shouted. "I told you it was the wrong field."

Ten minutes later the children found themselves in what are now termed 'customer facing positions.' That is, standing behind a table with instructions to sell something. Jessica was the star, but a career in retail does not beckon for my boys. Mind you, Ben did show clear potential for senior management by retiring to Jane's car to eat and drink, periodically sticking his head out of the window to ask, "How many pounds have we got?" Tom's incentive system wasn't far behind – every sale seemed to merit a drink, a sandwich or a 99.

We'd finally had enough by two o'clock. The only people buying off us now were the die-hard car booters, intent on making 50p mark up on a battered Postman Pat puzzle. We packed the cars ready for home. Twenty minutes and I'd be sitting in the garden with a cold beer.

"Mummy's waving at us," Jessica said as we set off.

"Wave back," I said. "I need a beer."

"It's not a nice wave. I think she's stuck."

Jane's car had paid the inevitable price of having

the tailgate open for seven hours. Interior light on, battery flat. No-one near us had any jump leads. "But I think there's a tool man on the market," someone said.

"Whereabouts?"

"Right over there, in that far corner." I sighed as my beer faded into the distance, and trudged off with the boys. "Why don't you and Jessica cash up?" I suggested to Jane.

We were back twenty minutes later. "How have we done?" I asked.

"Well…" Jane said, "We've got just over a hundred in the tin. But when you take off six quid each for the cars, float, shorts for Tom, drinks, sweets, your bacon sandwiches and wages for the children we've made nine pounds fifty. Anyway," she said cheerfully, "You found the jump leads."

I nodded. "They came with some gloves and a tow rope."

"How much?"

"Ten quid…"

The Bug With No Name

It was just like a Clint Eastwood movie. The Bug hit our house on Sunday afternoon. "I don't feel well," Ben had said that morning. What he meant was, "There's trouble heading our way."

You know how it goes. The stranger rides into town. Just to let everyone know he's there he shoots someone for laughing at his horse. It goes quiet for a while – "Too darn quiet," some fool usually says – then all hell breaks loose.

Five minutes after Ben's warning he was right as rain, we forgot all about it and he went off to visit his Gran for the day. "Has he had much to eat?" I asked Mum when I collected him.

"Not much," she said. "Beans on toast, an apple, an ice cream and some milk." Translated from the Granny-speak, that would be several glasses of milk with strawberry powder, two large ice creams and a bag of sweets.

Twenty minutes later we were sitting down to Sunday lunch. As usual when a meal was ready a child was missing. This time it was Ben. "Where is he?" I sighed.

"He's in the downstairs toilet," Jessica replied. "He's feeling – "

The unmistakable sound of Ben throwing up

finished the sentence for her. I raced to the toilet, just managing to dodge Jane with a plate of roast beef. Ben was sitting on top of the seat. A pool of vomit was in the corner of the room. "Why didn't you lift the seat up and be sick in the toilet, Ben?"

"It's broken," he sobbed. "It won't stay up." He was right – it was. Jane had been asking me to fix it for three weeks.

"Daddy?"

"What, treasure?"

"I'm going to – " A torrent of baked beans poured into my groin. Vomit dripped steadily on to my shoes. Stupidly I tried to catch it in my hands. Now even my watch was soaked. Jane put her head round the door. "Dinner's ready," she smiled. "You might as well come and eat it."

The downstairs toilet was declared a no-go zone – there may well be an opening for this column to be sponsored by a carpet cleaning company. We've put a sign up, like the ones on those remote islands where the Government once tested anthrax. 'No admittance for a hundred years.'

After that it went quiet again – but the final shoot-out was just around the corner. The Bug was biding its time. The phone rang on Tuesday afternoon. "This is school," a voice said. They never ring with good news do they?

A very pale Tom was collected and mayhem broke out. Within hours the Bug had done it's work and there were groaning victims all over the house. Tom was sick at three-thirty, Jessica at seven-forty. I followed at ten minutes to midnight. We were going down every four hours and ten minutes. A bug with a built in timer. What next?

"I feel dreadful," Jane said.

"You'll be sick at four in the morning," I muttered from the bathroom floor. "Can't wait," she moaned and pushed me out of the way.

So what did we have? The medical profession call them "non-specific viruses." Whatever, it struck us all. The Bug With No Name achieved what Chinese flu, Spanish tummy and the common cold had never managed – it flattened all five of us. There was only one thing for it. With what little strength I had left I dialled my Mum's number. Maybe Gran could look after the children while Jane and I clung on to our buckets.

"Mum?"

"I can't talk to you," she said. "I'm going to be sick…"

What's in a Name?

I was tidying up the other day – no, it's not a misprint – and I came across the Baby Names book. It was well thumbed nine or ten years ago, but it's ready for the scrapheap now.

"Over 3,000 names to choose from," it proudly proclaimed. Right, that's always assuming you'd consider Acantha (it's Greek for sharp-pointed or thorny – charming), Aglaia, Abelard and Achilles as serious runners. And that's just the "A"s – in truth there aren't that many names to choose from are there? No wonder everyone's making up their own.

Jane and I had pretty well decided on 'Tom' from the time we started thinking about children. We didn't have a clue for number two though. We'd stroll romantically by the sea, pushing Tom in his pram and discussing girl's names. There was a time when we were on countries. "Do you like China?" I asked. "India," Jane replied. "I think India's a pretty name."

Those were the days when I'd agree to anything. If Jane wanted it, India was fine. "What about a second name?" I said. "I've always liked Kate."

We walked on, both of us wondering what it would be like to have two children. "India Kate," I said dreamily. "That sounds lovely."

"India Kate when you're turning right?" Jane

replied, "I don't think so, sweetheart."

By the time Ben arrived we'd spent so much time deciding whether to stick at two or go for three (no, we didn't check how much the cost of family holidays increased) that we settled on his name in about thirty seconds. "What do you think?" Jane said. It didn't give him embarrassing initials, it sounded OK if you shouted it down the garden – co-incidentally the same test I applied to the cat's name. "Fine with me," I said, and went back to clearing up the mess the first two had made.

There was another section of the book we looked at occasionally. Sandwiched neatly between the last girl's name – Zulema – and Aaron was 'Your baby's horoscope.'

'When the baby's due' is almost the first thing you learn, so you know the star sign before you know the sex. We thought Tom would probably be a Virgo – the book was very encouraging. "Considerate, helpful, popular, highly intelligent." Goodness me this parenting lark was going to be easy. I'd always believed in astrology.

Unfortunately Tom had different ideas – it was warm and cosy in there so he was eleven days late. Both the boys are therefore Librans. So how did the book score?

"Libran children realise that gurgles and smiles will get them anywhere in life." Tom nil, Ben one. "They dislike sticky fingers and cannot remain in a mess for long." What? I had to re-read that one – minus ten for both of them. That apart Ben scores pretty highly – good communicator, appreciates other people's feelings. It seems to have missed completely with Tom, but then it's probably not talking about the Libran child who's two years from being a teenager.

Jessica is a Leo – children who are supposed to be the Zodiac's greatest actors and entertainers. One point. If they can't get their way they'll throw a show-stopping drama instead. Right again. 'When they can't win at games they may become rebellious.' That would be another way of saying that the Monopoly board flies through the air would it? Spooky. But eventually I'm promised that Jessica will spread 'enormous fun and happiness throughout my life.' That'll do for me.

It'll have to, because it's unlikely that we'll have any more – I think that's what Jane means by "Absolutely no chance…"

Black and Blue Belt

The problem is, he can now hit me remarkably hard and I've got the bruises to prove it. This is my youngest we're talking about – Lethal Weapon 5.

Looking back over these columns I see that Ben started a 'little ninjas' course in October last year. The standing order that I cheerfully agreed to – confident it would be a passing fad and I wouldn't be paying out for more than a month or so – is still being collected. Ben is now a stripy-purple belt and takes every opportunity to prove it by kicking me.

It's an essential part of being a father that you have the occasional play fight with your children. Tom was straightforward. Punch, block, punch, block. Throw the occasional mock-punch back, let him catch you with one – it didn't hurt – wrestle a bit, collapse on the sofa, have a beer.

Ben is an entirely different proposition. We bow to each other. He attacks. Punch, front kick, reverse punch, punch with the other hand. Block – desperately – try and fight back. Here he comes again, snap punch, roundhouse kick, block, block again, ouch... Not only is he co-ordinated, he's learned to punch – properly.

And he's into surprise attacks. If you've seen a *Pink Panther* film it's like living with Cato. Making some toast? Whack. Go through a door without checking first? Punch, kick. Start shaving without scouting the bathroom first? Don't even think about it.

So now we have some pads, which I put on my hands – and he can punch and kick away to his heart's content. And he's got a cute little punchbag that he uses to practice his sparring. The trouble is that nothing quite matches the appeal of a live target – and you know who that means.

The person we have to thank for all this is Miss Smith – Ben's teacher. I think she's seventeen. Were I a 19 year old boy I would simply go and camp in her garden until she agreed to marry me. Is she good looking? Yes. Can she cook? Who knows. Can she control twenty screaming six year old boys? Like nothing you have ever seen. Of course, the fact that she could chop you into small pieces with one blow of her left hand is a bit of a drawback, but on balance you'd have to say it was a risk worth taking.

Not only has she shown Ben enough moves to qualify him as a one man combat unit she's also taught him 'focus.' He's there in his karate suit, impossibly long belt almost touching the floor, staring straight ahead. "Hi, Ben," she says. "How are you today?" No response. She tickles him – nothing. All around small boys are losing their concentration. A foam club suddenly crashes into the mat with a terrifying whack. I fall off my chair – Ben remains unmoved. Pretty soon he's last man standing and there's another 'Great Job' sticker on his suit.

For a while I had him convinced that he couldn't beat me as I'd studied under the venerable master

Tsing Tao. Sadly, Tom rumbled me on our last visit to the Chinese restaurant.

"Hey, Dad."

"What is it, Tom?"

"Why is this beer made by your martial arts teacher?"

We've another bout scheduled in a few minutes. I can cope with him punching me – it's the ones that land off target that I worry about. I'm just sneaking into the attic before we start. I want to dig out my old cricket kit – didn't think I'd ever need my box again...

Flat Broke

I was quietly minding my own business on the computer when Tom started hammering on the window.

"I've got a flat tyre."

"You can't have. It was your birthday on Thursday – you've only had your bike two days."

"Come and see."

I sighed, and went to look. So he had. I grabbed the bicycle pump and attacked it. No good. "Where's that trendy new pump we bought?" I asked. Neither of us could remember, so I searched upstairs and Tom went downstairs. When I came back he was pumping away. "It was in the lounge, Dad." Of course it was.

Still no progress. "Unscrew the pump and let me look at the valve," I said. In two years time I won't be able to get away with rubbish like that, but for now he still believes I know what I'm talking about. The damn thing wouldn't unscrew. "Let me have a go," I said, but it was no use. Thirty minutes later we wheeled the new bike back into the shop with one flat tyre and the bicycle pump stuck like a limpet to the back wheel.

The owner of the shop looked exactly like the owner of a bike shop should look. Trim, fit, efficient, knowledgeable and used to dealing with men who can't unscrew a pump. "No problem," she said. "I'll look at it after lunch." I gave her our phone number and went home for a sandwich.

I was out when the call came through. Jane phoned the mobile. "Puncture," she said. "You can collect it while you're in town – and she says she's going to show you how to take a wheel off." Jane has seen me try to put furniture together – she could barely speak for laughing.

The bike was indeed ready. Three days after I'd paid a fortune for it, so was a repair bill. "And you'll need a new pump," Mrs. Bike said, showing me the mangled remains of ours. Apparently Tom had screwed it straight on to the valve, without using the little connector tube. No doubt I'd have done the same thing at eleven, and quite possibly at a good deal older. "There's this," she said, showing me a pump exactly like the one we'd just trashed. "Or there's this one." She hoisted the bicycle pump to rule them all on to the counter. It looked like it would inflate a hot air balloon. I haven't a clue what pressure my car tyres are supposed to be, so the fact that it came with a pressure gauge seemed a shade irrelevant but it looked so awesome that I handed over the credit card for another thrashing.

I turned to go. "Hang on," Mrs. Bike said. "I promised your wife I'd show you how to change a wheel."

"Right," I said, wondering if this constituted unreasonable behaviour on Jane's part.

"It's really simple." It always is in the shop. "You just unclip the brake shoe, release the cam, loosen

143

the tension nut, slip the chain of the rear derailleur, and the wheel comes off." Of course it does. "Then – if you get another puncture – you can change the inner tube and pop the wheel back on." Assuming I'd suddenly passed my City & Guilds in Tour de France maintenance.

As soon as I got home Tom and Jessica went on a bike ride together. Would you believe it, they had an argument half way round. "No way, never, I am not going with her ever again."

"Well, you're just a freak and you can't keep up either, so there."

Lovely – we've a family bike ride planned for the weekend. I can't wait...

Losing my Grip?

Sometimes the whole thing just feels like it's slipping away doesn't it? Or does every other father have his children completely under control, his life perfectly in balance?

Right now Ben is refusing to do his spellings. Whatever his teacher claims I don't believe copying equals learning. He's also insisting that eating a bag of chocolate buttons is an integral part of the educational process. Jessica's stormed off to her bedroom. Apparently I said something but don't ask me what it was. No wonder men go to their garden sheds.

There's another ten or twelve years of this stretching ahead of me and I feel like I'm losing control. I'm strongly tempted to say, "OK, do what you like. Have a fight if you want, don't bother tidying your bedrooms, don't worry if your teeth drop out because you haven't brushed them, just leave me in peace."

But you can't. So you go to bed with a headache, wake up with one and have an argument with your wife somewhere in between. Maybe we should re-introduce the rule we had when Tom kept us awake all night teething – nothing we said to each other between going to bed and getting up counted in the morning.

What Jane and I need is a romantic weekend away. We've been planning one for about three years now. When we eventually make it we'll have forgotten why we planned it in the first place. But we can't go next weekend because Jessica's in the cross country, then Ben has his ninja grading exam. Then it's Christmas – and isn't Tom doing something in the New Year? And so it goes on – and then it's so close to the summer holiday that it's hardly worth bothering...

But it's our computer that's really made me feel I'm losing it. The machine is now terminally ill and a replacement is long overdue. The monitor and all the other stuff is fine, so I'm reliably informed we need a "box only" system.

By the time I've looked at those big fat mags full of computer-speak I'm hopelessly confused, so I waved the white flag and asked Tom to type out the spec for me. I faxed it off to the local computer shop and they duly faxed back a price – around £200 more than the budget. On Saturday morning I marched in with Tom – and several pages of his notes – in an attempt to remove the extra £200. A young man who was far more knowledgeable about computers than he was about washing his hair appeared. He proceeded to have a long conversation with Tom while I stood helplessly by. If they'd been speaking Latvian I'd have been just as well informed.

"To be honest the size of the graphics card isn't as important as the chip set."

"But we need to balance the CPU with the chip set."

"That's why you need an AMD 64 3000+. A

Sempron is cheap but it won't improve performance – it's just a pared down Athlon."

Fortunately we'd taken Ben with us – so I had a nice chat with him about the Christmas tree lights in the shop.

Inevitably the villain of the piece turned out to be the new licensing rules from Microsoft. We managed to knock a bit off the price – but then the machine would be obsolete again in nine months. I left the shop with the distinct feeling I'd be negotiating with Jane – not something to look forward to with Christmas shopping round the corner. Now I come to think of it there's some work needs doing in the garden shed...

Does he Exist?

So – does he or doesn't he? With every passing year it's getting more and more difficult to convince Ben that Father Christmas really is setting off from the North Pole. I'm a big believer in keeping the magic of childhood alive as long as possible, but when you've an older brother and sister, it's an uphill struggle for Mum and Dad.

I'm pretty certain the problem is Jessica – she's just too shrewd is that girl. I'm not sure she's ever believed in Santa and she's known the importance of a PIN number since she was about two. "Don't worry if you forget it, Daddy," she told me. "I've got it written down." Tom, on the other hand, will believe in anything as long as it guarantees the arrival of an Xbox.

"Father Christmas is coming to school next week," Ben told me yesterday.

"Is he? All the way from the North Pole – that's lovely."

"Not the real one, Dad – a teacher."

"Don't be silly, there's only one Father Christmas."

Ben sighed. "So how did he know exactly what I wanted last year? Because you and Mummy bought it."

It's the trips to town that are the big problem – when you can meet three Santas in five minutes. "Learners,

Ben. Then they'll have a competition one day to see which one will take over when the real one retires."

And what about that other mystery personality – the Tooth Fairy? Here we have a complete reversal. Tom thinks it's complete madness. He regularly clashes with his headmaster over God versus the Big Bang, so the idea of a fairy with a collection of teeth strikes him as too stupid to contemplate. But Jessica will happily accept any old rubbish if we're adding another pound to her collection. Poor old Ben's still skewered – but right now he's listening to Tom.

"It's you, Dad, I know it is."

"I haven't got a pound. I spent it all on chocolate…"

"Mummy gave it to you," he said. "Mummy gives you all your money." What? Thanks for that vote of confidence.

And so I go on, trying to blend truth and fiction. The video shop was seriously lacking in the PG department last week, so the family film was *Van Helsing*. And of course, when they were going to bed we had to explain. No, Ben, werewolves don't exist, and there's no such thing as vampires either. But, yes, Father Christmas and the Tooth Fairy are real – and that's my entirely logical position.

But for a boy, the suspension of rational belief is pretty vital in later life. How depressed would I have been as a teenager if I hadn't clung to the belief that Angela Miller would kiss me one day? It was the only thing that kept me going through double Maths. She finally agreed to go out with me – after she'd tried everyone else in my class. I blew six weeks of my part time wages on taking her to the Italian. Stupidly

I ordered spare ribs – the only food you eat like a beaver gnawing a tree trunk. No matter – any second she'd announce that her parents were away for the weekend. Then I caught sight of myself in one of the restaurant mirrors. There were rivers of blood red barbecue sauce running from my mouth to my ears. Angela had noticed too. "I couldn't possibly kiss you," she said. "You look like a vampire with a bit of dead pig stuck between its teeth."

So that's the wisdom I'm passing on to my boys this week. Father Christmas is alive and well – and if you're on a hot date, stick to the pasta...

True Confessions

This is the sort of thing I usually keep to myself, but – at the risk of guaranteeing my removal to a secure rest home – here it is. I was raking through the bottom of my wardrobe on Christmas Eve, looking for the book I was certain I'd bought for my Mother. I came across a bag I hadn't seen before. Looking inside I found a brand new pair of shoes. They were my size, and exactly what I needed for work. "Well," I thought, "Fancy Jane buying me a pair of shoes for Christmas. Not your normal Xmas present but just what I wanted. Thanks, love."

I was hugely impressed by her ingenuity in hiding them in my own wardrobe – the one place she could normally be certain I wouldn't look. She'd left the price ticket on them as well – a lot more than I usually spent on shoes.

But the more I thought about it, the more I couldn't believe it. Shoes? It simply wasn't a Jane type of present. And the more the alternative solution bothered me. It didn't take Sherlock Holmes to work out that if Jane hadn't bought them, I had – and then I'd put them at the bottom of my wardrobe and completely forgotten about them.

In the end I couldn't resist asking her. "Er, have you bought me anything to wear this year?"

"Not since you took the last three jumpers back."

"Nothing to wear on my feet?"

"I'd rather not think about your feet," she said coldly. "Anyway, why do you ask?"

I told her, trying not to be too embarrassed. "You can't remember buying them?" Jane's eyes glinted. Suddenly next Christmas looked a good deal simpler. All she had to do was start looking in my wardrobe – say, from July onwards – and take away any new clothes she found.

Then on Christmas Day she lovingly gives them to me as presents – they haven't cost her a penny, and I'm really impressed because they're exactly what I wanted.

Now she patiently explained that we'd been to Carlisle about six months ago to visit friends. She was right. We had – it all came flooding back to me.

Clothes play a marginally less important part in my life than the Uruguayan short-course swimming championships. Younger women, whose boyfriends can cheerfully spend £100 on a shirt, may find this unbelievable. Women who've been married for any length of time will wonder why it's taken me so long to confess.

But once a year I suddenly have an urge to shop, and this year it happened in Carlisle. Now I remembered marching into M&S. In their sizes I'm XL at the top, 36/33 at the bottom and shoe size 43. So there is absolutely no need to shop anywhere else. My list consisted of two pairs of work trousers and some new black shoes. To Jane that's not even a warm up lap but to me it's a major shopping expedition.

And pretty soon that was me done for another year.

At least I thought it was until Tom came running up to me at the check out. "Can I have these, Dad?"

I looked at him in astonishment. In one hand he held a dark blue shirt, in the other some trousers. "Do you want those?" I asked stupidly.

"I thought they looked cool."

"You've chosen them yourself?"

He looked at me as though I was mad. "Of course I have. I like buying clothes."

Now there's something else to worry about. Do I wait twelve months to see if it was Tom's annual shopping urge? Or do I demand an immediate paternity test...

You, Me, the Kids

Well, it's been 2005 for eleven days now, and so far –
you won't believe this – I'm in the lead. Like everyone
I know, we've got one of those kitchen calendars
divided into three – 'You,' 'Me,' and the section which
is always full to bursting, 'the Kids.'

Tom was complaining to me the other day. "It's
not fair," he moaned, (there's a surprise). "I haven't
had a sleepover for at least six months."

I dug out last year's calendar to check. As usual,
Tom's memory proved to be highly selective – but as
I flicked through the pages, an interesting picture of
last year started to emerge.

Ben's life largely consisted of going to ninjas,
attending birthday parties and having friends round.
Jessica was the clear winner in the sleepover stakes,
and as the most sporty of our three had a glut of cross
country races, netball tournaments and anything else
that involved me standing on the touchline wishing
I'd worn a thicker coat. Tom comfortably captured
the school trip trophy. It must be year five going into
year six. There didn't seem to be a week when he
wasn't off on another educational visit – always with
a couple of quid of my spending money in his pocket.

Sadly, if you believed everything you read on the
calendar, Jane's social life was made up of work-do's

and waiting for Tesco deliveries. She did go out for a meal with her mates once. It was March 11th if you must know, so I suppose she's due for another one fairly soon. According to the calendar though, the rest of her year was spent bleakly waiting for the fortnightly delivery of carrier bags. I must have lost my grip over Christmas because I foolishly mentioned this to her. "I'd noticed," she said grimly, and took hold of the stick I'd given her and started to beat me with it.

Mind you, I did even worse. I scoured last year in vain looking for the four day golf trip to Portugal that might have slipped my memory. So when I jotted down another exciting appointment – optician, Saturday 22nd – I was elated to find myself in the lead for this year. Strictly speaking it was Jane and I that had been invited out on January 1st and 2nd – but so what, the entries were in my column.

Inevitably the children are back at school now – so any moment I'm going to be returned to my familiar last place. Tom's even starting guitar lessons this term. He might not be the next Eric Clapton – not if he's my son – but it's more ammunition for the 'kids' column. There's swimming for Ben, and Jessica will be weighing in with the full monty of sport. So it looks like Mum and Dad's taxi is back from it's mid-winter break, if it ever had one.

Anyway, even when you do go out, what do you find? The same exhausted parents you see at school. And what do we all talk about? Our children. Sad doesn't begin to describe it.

So why is it that summer camps have never caught

on in this country? I watched Homer and Marge wave their children off the other night. Bart and Lisa were going to Kamp Krusty for six weeks. Six weeks! With only Ben at home and a bit of co-operation from Granny that could be like three honeymoons, one after the other. But I suppose we'd miss them – and besides, after being a parent for eleven years, I'm not sure I'd have the energy for one more honeymoon, never mind three...

The Chains Come Off

It looks like we've finally decided that the children aren't going to drink the bleach. "You know," Jane said to me, "I think it's time we took the child-locks off the cupboards."

To be honest, I hadn't even realised they were still there. That's just how you open a cupboard in our house – pull the door, put your hand in, push the little safety catch out of the way, then open it up. If Jane hadn't pointed it out the safety catches would still have been there when Tom brought his first girlfriend home from college – even more embarrassing than showing her the photos of him as a baby.

Not that I had much to do with fitting the wretched catches on the cupboards – another example of my hopeless inability at DIY. "There you are," I said to Jane as baby Tom crawled round our ankles. "He won't get into that one."

"Right…" she said doubtfully as Tom opened the door and stuck his head inside. "Shouldn't the bit on the door and the locking thingy on the side line up?" Not for the last time an exploded diagram with no words had completely outwitted me. Jane's Dad was newly retired, so when I came home from work the next day he'd humiliated me by instantly turning the house into Fort Knox.

Getting a tin of soup was hard enough, but going from the kitchen to our bedroom had suddenly become a trial by combat. Baby gates were everywhere – even at the entrance to the kitchen (I think that was to stop Tom eating the cat food). There was one at the bottom of the stairs, and the de-luxe version – copied from Alcatraz if I'm not mistaken – waiting at the top.

If you eventually made it to the bedroom and wanted to open a window that was too bad. We had window locks designed by a mechanical engineering genius who'd very possibly died before telling anyone else how to open them.

How a child that could only just crawl was supposed to scale the bedroom wall and tip himself out of the window I'm still not sure, but you know what it's like with your first baby. Anxious or what? If Boots were selling something to guarantee that Elvis couldn't come down in an alien space ship and abduct him we bought six of them.

But the gates were my real enemy. Despite being made for children they weren't short of sharp corners. I came sprinting downstairs one day to watch England winning a test match – when it was the exception, not the rule – and pushed the gate open too quickly. The gate, and the medieval spike that locked it, bounced back at exactly the right moment to impale my thigh. Half an inch to the left and future discussions about a vasectomy would have been irrelevant.

Still, the house is now free of all restrictions and according to my calculations we're entering a golden age where we don't have to worry about security – at least for eighteen months. Then we'll be sifting through the books to check what we don't want Tom to read – and then one day I'll come home to find the last beer mysteriously absent, Tom playing poker on the internet and know it's all downhill from there.

I was chatting to my brother last week. His children are much older than mine, and he'd been to a wedding where my nephew was best man.

"I met some of Phil's friends," he said, clearly still shell-shocked. "They told me about all the wild parties they'd had at our house when we'd been away."

"Thanks," I thought. There's something else to look forward to…

Bottom Gear

Here's what I know about cars: they have wheels, they run on petrol and the children turn them into travelling dustbins. Oh, and these days – unlike the little white mini I had when I was twenty – if there's surface water on the road it won't spray up through a hole in the floor and hit you in the face.

But that's it. Cars have absolutely no interest for me. I point my car at Newcastle, say "Go" and it takes me there. That'll do for me. How the petrol gets turned into the power to drive the car I don't know – and I don't want to know.

I'm aware that this makes me different to the vast majority of men, but so what? When I was fifteen people suddenly started coming to school wearing anoraks with stripes down the sleeve and 'Castrol' on their left breast. How they could find a car more interesting than football, cricket and Angela Miller I've never been able to understand.

So why are Tom and Jessica fascinated by *Top Gear?* "Come on," I said last Sunday, "Let's all watch this together – there's a programme about sharks." Not surprisingly the children yawned loudly – if you've enough channels you can just about watch sharks 24/7 these days.

"Bedtime," I said when they'd endured it. "School

tomorrow."

"No," they screamed, and went completely mad.

"What do you mean 'no'?"

"It's *Top Gear*. Please, Dad, please. We'll go straight to bed afterwards. Please – we'll even brush our teeth without being told."

Who wants to watch *Top Gear* when they can see *Sky Sports News* on freeview? Especially with the league table regularly flashing up to confirm that 'Pools are still there, cruising in fifth place. My children, that's who.

"Why do you like it?" I asked.

"Jeremy's funny."

"I'm funny…"

"Not deliberately, Dad. Besides, he bought a car for £100 last week."

"So what? I've bought a car for £100."

For once they were impressed by their father. That's exactly what my mini cost me – a few years ago admittedly. That car did have certain endearing qualities. I took a girlfriend out in it once. The heater was broken and the car was so cold she had to wrap her feet in newspaper. Oddly, the relationship didn't last.

You already know about the automated face washing system, and on cold winter nights I had to put a blanket on the engine. I forgot about it once and drove to Sunderland with the blanket still under the bonnet – it made no difference. Worst of all, if it rained the car would only start if I spent five minutes rubbing the points with an old pair of underpants.

Still, it did give me the highlight of my formative

years – I'd finally made some progress in my eternal pursuit of Angela Miller by giving her a lift home. The fan belt broke and I managed to persuade her the only way to fix it was to use her tights.

Poor old Tom. I feel sorry for him really. His first car will be some boring, ultra reliable German or Japanese thing. There'll be 100,000 miles on the clock and it will still go on for ever. He'll never know that moment of pure, blind terror when the mechanic sucks his breath in and shakes his head – and you know the repair bill's a lot more than your overdraft limit.

There'll be no holes in the floor, no rubbing the points with his old pants – and worst of all, no chance of convincing Angela Miller's daughter that it's the fan belt and there's only one solution...

Our Computer – RIP

"We need a new graphics card as well, Dad"

"Why?"

"For the shadows. And the colours."

"What will that do?"

"Well, before the game was red and blue, but a good graphics card will make it ruby and sapphire."

That's a big difference isn't it? Well worth sixty quid of anyone's money. I phoned the shop and accepted the terms of my surrender.

After several months of fighting off Tom's pleas for a new computer, the wretched machine took his side last week by dying. I turned it on, it blinked at me a couple of times – and then it made the same pathetic groaning noise I do when I have a hangover. And that was that. Jane, Tom and I sat and stared at it for several minutes, but no amount of collective will power would bring it back to life.

We all had an acute case of DCS – dead computer syndrome. I hadn't realised, but if I want to know anything at all these days I simply ask Google. I've lost the ability to look in a book. There's a Reality TV show in this as well – *Computer Swap*, the children's version of *Wife Swap*. In the first programme Tom spends two weeks with a family that consider a Commodore 64 to be perfectly adequate and don't own an Xbox.

It turned out to be the motherboard, otherwise known as a hundred quid. That was to restore it to the old status quo – slow, clunky and in Tom's opinion not much good for anything beyond a game of solitaire. To bring it into the current millennium required rather more – six weeks after Xmas is not exactly the best time to find a spare £350. "It's a bit like a heart transplant," John the computer man said. "The new parts will reject the old ones."

Tom couldn't have had better news. I waved the white flag and my son dived into three inch thick computer magazines to scour incomprehensible lists of parts. Did I want his opinion? It didn't matter, I was going to get it.

We ended up with a new motherboard, processor, sound card and several other things I didn't understand. Tom ended up with a large box full of second hand parts – begged off the computer shop. His bedroom has now transformed itself into an engineer's workshop – every available surface is covered. You can still see the carpet, but it's only a matter of time. I collected football cards when I was his age – maybe motherboards are the modern equivalent.

Anyway the computer is back. It's fast, it's quiet, and in my opinion it's haunted.

"Leave it on will you?" I said to Jane yesterday. "I just need to check something." I touched the keyboard and I swear a voice inside the computer shouted "Help me." Then it made a deep, growling noise. I tried to keep calm and carried on – until a witch started laughing at me.

"The computer's demonically possessed," I told Jane when she came back in.

She treated me to her most condescending look. "You've been outwitted by technology again, dear. Watch this," she said, and went on to her buddy list. Every one of them had a noise attached. How was I to know that AOL let you tell people you're online by shouting, "Help me?"

"I'd never heard them because the old sound card wasn't good enough," I said. "That's money well spent, isn't it? Three hundred quid to be terrified every time I go online."

"Possibly," my wife said. "But you're forgetting one thing. You don't need to worry – you haven't any buddies…"

Compensation Culture

I can't even remember what he wanted, but I was pretty determined. "No," I said to Tom last week. "I can't afford it."

"Why not?" he asked.

Sometimes I come close to swearing at my eldest son. "Because I've just paid for an enormous computer repair, that's why," I said, staring glumly at my bank statement and trying to keep calm.

As usual, Tom wouldn't be deterred so easily. "Why don't you get a loan, Dad?" he asked.

"I don't want a loan, thanks."

"But on the TV they say you can have a loan for whatever you want."

Right at that minute a loan to fund someone to take over child care seemed highly attractive. Like everyone else I could always put it down as home improvements. I was about to launch into the perils of borrowing when Jessica wandered in. She'd obviously heard the conversation.

"You can have the money tomorrow, Dad. The adverts say so."

"For the last time," I said, "I don't want a loan."

"Yes, you do," Jessica said, "Then you could consolidate it – whatever that means."

And if that didn't prove that the children had

watched too much daytime TV during half term, nothing did. I read somewhere that 60% of all bankrupts are now under the age of 30 – hardly surprising is it? I don't wish to sound like a grumpy old man – which I am – but I am slightly worried that we're rearing a generation of children whose idea of financial planning is to take out a loan, take out another one, consolidate the first two and then pay it off one day with compensation.

The eldest two are now specialists in compensation payments – they've turned into lawyers overnight. There's no need to worry about tuition fees if they ever go to Law School – all they have to do is watch the ads for a fortnight. Tom's currently studying under that very plausible lady who pops up on *Sky Sports News* every time you want to check on the league tables. I think he's about ready to launch his business.

"Have your parents forced you to eat your vegetables? Been sent to your bedroom unfairly? You may be entitled to compensation. Ring 'Children-watching-too-many-adverts' now. No salesman will call and your parents need never know." Until they're forking out the compo that is.

They know their rights as well. Jessica threatens to call Childline so often I'm thinking of adding the number to 'Friends and Family'. Have I ever infringed her basic human rights? Absolutely. I found her guilty without trial, and she was falsely imprisoned in her bedroom. I denied her fundamental right to watch *Tracey Beaker* and refused leave to appeal. What's more if she nips Ben like that again I'll do the same tomorrow.

What about parents' human rights? The basic right to open a beer, sit down and watch the football – in peace. I tried to see two games at the weekend. In between breaking-up fights, sorting out whose turn it was on the computer and Jane threatening me with a list of jobs, I missed every single goal.

I'd finally managed ten uninterrupted minutes when Jessica came downstairs wailing.

"What's the matter?" I asked her.

"I tripped over my trackie bottoms and banged my knee."

"How did you trip over your trackie bottoms?"

"They were on my bedroom floor."

"Well, it's your own stupid fault then. You should have tidied them up."

"No, Dad. It's your fault. You haven't taught me to tidy my room properly."

And given the state of the compensation laws these days, she's probably right. Where's my cheque book…

Freezing Point

Not exactly the best time for it to happen, but our central heating broke down last week. The system had been making more than it's fair share of clunks and groans for a while, but somehow we'd never got round to having it serviced. Perhaps it was the size of the estimate and associated increase in the mortgage that made us rely on prayers instead.

The trouble was, they weren't answered. Just as the weather warnings were flashing across the screen, Jessica came downstairs to report that her bedroom was "Way freezing." Ben soon followed. Tom didn't say anything – he simply went to bed in his coat. Our room was no better. Jane came to bed wearing a cardigan and socks. I didn't bother making any romantic suggestions.

I spent the next morning on the phone to plumbers. More precisely, I spent the morning leaving messages on answerphones. One of them might be returned one day. Eventually I found a plumber's wife at home and persuaded her to part with her husband's mobile number. He answered on the fourth ring. Easy, I thought. Straight back into Jane's good books.

I explained the problem. "Alright," he said grudgingly. "I can come and have a look."

"Brilliant," I gasped in relief. "When?"

"I'm a bit booked up. Then I'm on holiday. First week of May any good to you?"

I can't tell you what Jane said when I reported back. So where do you find a plumber? As far as I can tell there are now more people working as Elvis Presley impersonators than plumbers. You need a middle aged bloke in a white suit and sideburns to nip round and sing *Heartbreak Hotel?* They're coming out of the woodwork. Want your central heating fixing? Last week you had more chance of Elvis himself turning up with the wrench.

You would therefore be right to assume that marital relations in our house are a bit strained. 'Frosty' is a serious understatement. The children don't like me much either. I'd have thought that after all these years they'd have learned that the words 'Dad' and 'Fixed it' very rarely appear in the same sentence. Perhaps it's time I went back to school – maybe a City and Guilds in Advanced Plumbing is what I've been missing all these years.

All this has set me thinking though – when I'm warm enough to think that is. What sort of careers advice should you give your children? It's not something we've really discussed with our three, although you'd get long odds against computers not appearing somewhere on Tom's CV. But everyone else is in danger of being replaced by a micro chip or a hologram by the time my children are at work – so what do I tell them? I have serious doubts about the traditional approach of further education and a sensible job. Maybe it's time to go back to learning a trade. If present trends continue this country will end up with a million media studies graduates and two dozen plumbers.

So if Jessica doesn't become President of the World Bank, she'll be available to fix your heating in about ten years time. And even if she is President, I shall still tell her to marry a plumber – especially if his brother's an electrician, his Dad's a joiner and his mate does building work.

After all, the plumber's going to make more money. I cannot tell you the obscenely large amount that Jane said she'd pay to be warm again. Mind you it's nothing to what I'd shell out to stop her coming to bed dressed like my Granny...

Upwardly Mobile

"So, where shall we go this year?"

No answer.

"Greece?"

"Too hot."

"Spain?"

"Went last year."

"Somewhere in England?"

"Too wet."

"So where do you want to go on holiday?"

The answer – if Tom and Jessica were left to make the decision – would be Carphone Warehouse. Right now a week spent looking at mobile phones seems to be their idea of Heaven. Somewhere hot with a pool and a vat of cold beer is so far down the list it's out of sight.

Needless to say it's my fault. I finally upgraded my mobile last week, setting off a surge of envy in Tom and Jessica. Suddenly they've reached the age where they're obsessed with the latest mobiles. They endlessly discuss photos, videos, flip phones, screensavers – and above all, does it look 'cool?' Tom currently spends more time on nokia.com than he does on destroying aliens. He's got his own mobile – so has Jessica – but neither of them are exactly state of the art. To be fair, I think Jessica has my original

Nokia 1. Now, of course, the race is on to get their hands on the new one.

The rule so far has been simple. If either Jane or I upgrade, Tom and Jessica take it in turns to have the old mobiles. Jane's due to upgrade soon, and Jessica's next on the list. The trouble is, Jane's mobile has received the dreaded thumbs-down – it's "way uncool." Jessica maintains she has the right to waive her turn and wait for mine. Tom – fairly forcibly – says she doesn't. This one is heading straight to the House of Lords.

Why do they want my new phone so badly? It takes photos, but that's a given these days. It shoots videos, surfs the internet and sends e-mails. It can download half the world's computer programmes, and it's so clever that I can be watching 'Pools and use the phone to put a bet on them – unless they're playing Wrexham that is.

Naturally, it's all completely wasted on me, the man whose ring tone is still 'ring ring.' I've taken some not-bad photos of the children, but as I haven't mastered keypad-lock yet I've also taken a riveting picture of the inside of my pocket. Heaven help me when we reach the Japanese level, where you use your mobile to pay for the shopping. Perhaps I should tell Jane to stock up now.

And if everything's going to be ordered by text, I'm in even more trouble. Anything over ten characters and I give up and hand the phone to Jessica. Predictive text? You must be joking.

I heard somewhere that the Government think reading and writing won't be key skills in 15 years time. Looking at some of the text messages I get from my children I'd say that was a serious overestimate. Is it now actually illegal for someone under the age of 16 to spell a word correctly in a text message?

Then again, as a certain right-sided midfielder can testify, mobiles can get you into even deeper water. I was watching Jessica in a cross country the other day. "Lend me your phone, Dad," she said. "I want to take a photo." I was too numb with cold to protest, so I meekly handed it over. Next time I looked my wallpaper had been replaced with a photo of Miss Luscious, Jessica's 25 year old PE teacher. I haven't a clue how to change it back, and now Jane's convinced I'm having an affair. I should have the energy. Still, it's a thought to keep you warm as the snow drifts down...

Future Shock

"What about this one then?"

"Fine, Daddy. If you've just died."

"This one – this is nice."

"It's got checks on it, Dad." Jessica sighs patiently. "It's like, soooo unfashionable."

"How do you know?"

"Trust me. I'm a girl."

Eventually I find a shirt that my daughter approves of and we can move on. Just in time I remember to buy some flowers for my Mum. She was away on March 6th so Mother's Day was postponed to last Sunday. Three bunches, so the children can give their Gran one each – even if it does mean manhandling Tom off the computer and forcing him to be charming under pain of death.

And then Jessica blows it. "These are lovely," my Mum says.

"They are aren't they, Gran? And they were three bunches for £2." Jessica smiles at her. "Daddy was too mean to buy the expensive ones."

That's my nine year old daughter – humiliating me one minute, embarrassing me the next.

I was in Nottingham last week and stayed with my friend Liz. I hadn't seen her for about eight years and like everyone else I know she's divorced and remarried along the way. She has a stepson now, so there are two thirteen year olds – Evan and Rachel – in the house. As if I needed one, it was a sobering glimpse into the future.

Evan impressed me immediately. He ambled happily in from school carrying half a playing field on his trousers. Mud? That wasn't an adequate word. I was sorely tempted to take a photograph so that next time Jane was berating Tom I could show her my mobile and say, "Wait – it gets worse." Evan proceeded to eat half the food in the fridge and then disappeared to the computer in his bedroom, possibly for ever.

"I worry that he spends too much time on the computer," Liz said. That sounded vaguely familiar. "We can't get him downstairs for meals." You don't say. It struck me that Evan was Tom – just the next size up.

"He plays this online game where he wanders round trading wood and gold. I haven't a clue what's going on." Now we were entering the Twilight Zone. When Liz told me that she left Evan a note every day to remind him to shut his bedroom door I wondered if some bizarre birth accident had taken place. Maybe Evan and Tom were twins – separated by two years and two hundred miles.

Liz's daughter, Rachel, was six weeks older than Evan. It could have been six years. She floated round the house in a permanent state of cool.

"I think she's going to be a Goth," Liz said. Goths? They went to Whitby every year didn't they? "It's a sort of dark hippie," Liz explained. "I think it'll be OK."

I hadn't given much thought to what my children would be as teenagers. When Liz told me that the alternative for Rachel was hanging round the shopping centre in hipster jeans and thongs, becoming a Goth at thirteen didn't seem so bad. I tried chatting to her but Rachel had clearly decided I wasn't cool enough to speak to. Evan eventually surfaced and we cheerfully discussed nerdy things – while Rachel treated us to the condescending look that my lovely daughter has very nearly perfected.

Still I can see some compensations ahead. Jessica will undoubtedly follow suit and decide I'm "Soooo uncool" that she can't possibly speak to me, let alone be seen in my company. On current form I could be looking forward to several years of peace and quiet – and choosing my own shirts...

Head Lines

Jessica's current best friend is Claire. This was decidedly bad news when Claire's mother rang recently. "I'm sorry to tell you this," she said, "But Claire's got nits. She caught them off her cousin."

To be honest with you, Jane didn't care where she'd caught them. She did care that Jessica and Claire had been swimming the day before, and had then spent the rest of the afternoon lying side by side on Jessica's bed. All our three children were promptly lined up and examined. Nothing was found, but that didn't stop me spending the rest of the day scratching my head every twenty seconds.

So far – and I realise that even writing this down is a seriously foolish act – our house has been a nit-free zone. But apparently they're becoming increasingly immune to the shampoo you're supposed to use. No doubt they'll shortly find a way of mutating with GM crops and become totally invincible.

Anyone with children will be aware of nits. I'm old enough to remember the nurse turning up at school. We'd stand in a line while she raked through our hair and Mrs. Flood yelled at us to keep still.

These days all the school does is send out a letter – and you can put your mortgage on it arriving in the first week of term. The trouble is, it's always the same letter.

"We are sorry to report that there has been an incidence of head lice – sometimes called nits – at school. Combing with a fine tooth comb is the best remedy. Mrs. *(insert name of latest parent to be infected)* also tells us that *(insert name of most recent shampoo she's tried)* is very effective." Well she would, wouldn't she? Mrs. X isn't going to say, "We've tried everything and our family's still got them." No chance of her kids being invited for a sleepover.

If combing and shampoo isn't the answer, what is? Just in case I've tempted fate once too often, I've already done my research. Inevitably, Google was the starting point – a mere 16,100 entries to wade through. Amazon.com threw up an equally staggering number of books. Clearly my attempts to write a best-seller about a newspaper columnist struggling with his children have been totally on the wrong track.

I checked the first Google entry and discovered that at any one moment 12 million Americans have nits. No wonder there are three National Bug Busting Days on the US calendar – as far as I'm aware Christmas and Easter Sunday still only merit one day each over there.

As you might expect, the Americans are not messing about with shampoos and fine tooth combs. Here come the Weapons of Mass Destruction. First of all there's the electric zapper comb – as developed in the state of Texas and closely related to the cattle prod. You go through your child's hair and... bang! Every time the comb finds one of the little critters it's electrocuted. Inevitably there'll be a lawsuit happening right now with the person that tried to use the zapper comb in the shower.

They don't stop there though. For a bargain $9.99 you can buy a product called 'Neon Nits.' Spray it on your child's hair and the nits glow a luminous pink. Presumably you then lead your offspring into a darkened room and pick the things out at your leisure – something to look forward to on a wet Sunday afternoon.

So on balance I think we'll be keeping away from Claire for a while. Jessica can be difficult enough in the mornings without her wandering into our bedroom with pink highlights shimmering ominously in her hair. That would be a job for my wife, I think...

Slowhand

I woke up this morning
 Knew I had to go to school
 Forgotten to do my homework
 Man, I'm feeling such a fool

What's that? A 12 bar blues? Then again, what is a 12 bar blues? As you'll find out, I don't have a musical bone in my body.

Eric Clapton – sorry, Tom – had a birthday two months before Christmas. One of his presents was a guitar – a beginner's guitar with a beginner's price tag, thank goodness, as we'd agreed to pay for a few lessons as well. I was a tad sceptical. I assumed that since Tom looked like me and acted like me he'd have my musical ability – as detailed above. OK, he could sing well enough to be in the choir, but an instrument? I didn't think so.

Well, it's time to issue the official apology. He came home last week with his music report. "Very good progress, an excellent term's work that shows real promise." A large slice of humble pie, please.

All you can hear in our house now is the sound of him strumming away. Astonishingly the guitar has almost replaced the computer in his affections – that is, I've just found him playing guitar and computer game at the same time.

So, it looks like the music gene (along with the DIY gene and several other useful ones) has skipped me and landed on my children. Apparently it comes from my Grandfather, who was close to being a concert pianist. The story goes that his parents locked him in his room and refused to feed him until he'd done four hours practice every day.

Needless to say, I've now discovered some serious enthusiasm for Tom's guitar playing. I've stopped short of locking him in his bedroom, but I'm certainly encouraging the practice. After all, who's the only person that earns more than a Premiership footballer? A Rock Star.

I thought I'd help by letting him hear some proper guitar playing. Fortunately one of those *Monsters of Rock* freebie CDs flopped out of the paper, which saved me going up to the loft to rifle through some very old vinyl. Jimi Hendrix and *Purple Haze* seemed a good starting point. Tom listened for ten seconds and then fled. He couldn't have looked more disgusted if I'd suggested we live on sprouts for a week.

I can see some major clashes looming on the music front. I took Tom and Jessica shopping for new trainers at the weekend. Somehow we ended up in HMV – an increasingly powerful magnet. "Look at this," I said cheerfully, "All the ones that I like are only five quid."

Here came Little Miss Sarcastic again. "Right, Dad. That's because they're all dead."

She had a point, but the fact that all your musical heroes have died of excesses you never quite managed does have certain advantages when you're corralled into HMV. Presumably the CDs are so cheap because there are no more rock star lifestyles to maintain, just a bunch of flowers once a year. Or do the record companies know that we've all got children now and can't afford anything more than a fiver?

To be honest, I don't even need to spend that, given that the newspapers seem intent on meeting my musical needs for free. So I can happily yell *Bat out of Hell* to my heart's content in the car – or I could until Jessica decided it was 'gross' and replaced it with *Maggie May*.

Ben meanwhile, tells me that he wants to learn to play the drums – now there's something to look forward to. That sounds like the de-luxe ear plugs...

Illegal Tender

A dreadful scream of anguish rent the night air. (Sorry, I've been reading a cheap detective novel). It was Tom. I rushed in to the dining room where he was – no surprise – deeply into an online game. "What's happened?" I asked.

"I've been ripped off," he sobbed.

"What do you mean 'ripped off?'"

"I was trading some arrows." I'd rarely seen him so cross. "This…this…" Tom knew the word he wanted. He also knew that using it in the house wouldn't be a great career move. "This… He said he'd pay me 300,000." Whatever the currency was. "Then he cheated at the last minute. He only gave me 30,000."

I sympathised, but I could see a silver lining – another useful lesson in human nature. I don't want to bring the children up to believe the only friend they have is themselves, but hopefully they'll leave home with a healthy dose of scepticism. Tom's nature is to believe most things that he's told – even the fantasies of other eleven year old boys are reported as gospel truth – so if he gets exposed to the less savoury side of human nature before it costs him real money so much the better. If it seems too good to be true, Tom, it is too good to be true.

After all it won't be long before Angela Miller's daughter, Kylie, tells him she's washing her hair – for the fourth night in a row. Let's hope he's more perceptive than I was – I didn't really get the hint until Angie told me she'd rather take up stamp collecting.

We've been talking about human nature a lot recently – the trouble is, we seem to be concentrating on the nasty side of it. Jessica wandered into the dining room a couple of weeks after the Tsunami. "Dad, what does it mean when someone is selling children?" Before I could answer she fired off the other barrel. "And why do people steal the money that's been collected?"

I called Tom in as well. One meaningful discussion about right and wrong later I opened a beer with the smug satisfaction of a parent who – for once, at least – Had Done The Right Thing.

The next day I was in town with Tom and Jessica. Remembering the previous night I pointedly bought a *Big Issue*. And then I was ripped off.

Tom wanted to buy the latest PS2 game that was sweeping his school. As far as I could tell it was exactly the same as three or four other games we already had, but hey, what do I know? It was £29.99 and Tom was going to buy it with his own money.

"You're sure?" I'd said before we left home. He nodded. "Absolutely sure this is what you want? And you've got your own money?" I should have known better.

I still couldn't see the attraction of the game once we were in the shop, but Tom was determined. "Off you go then," I said, pointing at the till.

"Er…" My eldest hesitated.

"What's the matter?"

"I haven't exactly got the money…"

I sighed. "What have you got?"

Tom shuffled uneasily. "£10 of Waterstone's vouchers, five quid you owe me, £5 in cash and £10 in the bank."

"But the £10 in the bank's your savings…"

"Well I want to spend it."

"No way, Tom. You have to learn to save." So what happens? His face crumples, I weaken and my credit card is hit for £29.99. In return I receive a grubby five pound note and £10 worth of unwanted book tokens. Maybe it's me that needs to learn something…

Go On My Son

So what's your policy on alcohol? Let the children try it at any early age in the hope that they don't go mad when they're eighteen? (Or sixteen, fourteen, twelve as the case may be). Or do you say 'absolutely not,' cross your fingers and hope you never reap the whirlwind?

We've always taken the first approach. Tom's not interested in beer but he'll have the odd sip of wine. He 'quite likes it' but I suspect that's more to please us. Currently Jessica would quite happily drink strawberry milk for the rest of her life. And Ben? He's in the kitchen finishing off my beer, just like he's done since he was old enough to reach up and grab it.

And then there's gambling. At school I lurked ominously at the back of Mr. Davidson's Maths class, more interested in whether Rag Trade would win the Grand National (it did) than whether I would pass the quadratic equations exam (I didn't). Ever since, I've thought that most sporting events merit a small pecuniary interest. So on Saturday we turned our attention to this year's Grand National. The children were allowed two horses each, and I tried not to interfere. I explained the intricacies of win or each-way but Tom wasn't interested – he wanted to back the winner, and get the most money. Accordingly he went for Hedgehunter, the favourite, and Astonville, the rank outsider. I suggested that Astonville might well finish around Tuesday teatime but it was no use – at 500/1 he could almost taste a new computer.

I'd expected Jessica to go on names, or what she described as 'the prettiest uniform' (green, purple crossbelts, spotted cap). Instead, after twenty minutes studying the form, career earnings and the horses ages ("Our cats were quite old at 12, so that one can't possibly win") she plumped for Forest Gunner and – despite Tom's cries of 'copycat' – Hedgehunter.

Jane and Ben were happy to rely on names. The one name that had been on my list all week was Hedgehunter, but somehow I convinced myself that it wouldn't stay the trip and changed my mind. Instead I kept my fingers crossed for soft going and lumbered Strong Resolve and Marcus de Berlais with the responsibility of providing a long overdue set of new golf clubs.

Race time finally arrived and there we were, jostling for space on the settee. It turned out that I'd backed two greys – much easier to follow in the race, and sadly, much easier to see Strong Resolve all but fall at the first fence. Marcus plodded steadily along at the back like an elderly gentleman on a Sunday walk, so I was supporting the children's nags a lot sooner than I'd planned.

"Which is mine?"

"That one – on the inside. With the green cap."

"Innox, Innox, the man said mine."

"It's there, Ben. And look, Mum's jockey has fallen off…"

Jessica was starting to get excited with two in the first six, Tom had recovered from seeing his new computer pull up at the thirteenth and Ben was shouting at Innox. But it was all academic. No-one was going to catch Clan Royal...until the loose horse took a hand. Clan Royal refused, Hedgehunter hit the front, Jessica went ballistic and I started to feel sick.

Tom and Jessica were now side by side on the sofa, arms pumping as they rode their horse to victory. If anyone in our street is reading this I'm sorry about the hideous screaming. But it sounds an awful lot worse when you've deserted the winner and your children are demanding you settle up...

Perfect Citizens

By the time you're my age you pretty well have a subconscious routine for everything – even brushing your teeth. The same number of strokes in the same direction every day. For years I merrily brushed away on complete auto-pilot – then my children became 'environmentally aware.'

And suddenly, every time you want to rinse your toothbrush, they've turned the water off. Yes, I know they're right, I know they're saving the planet's resources and I'm squandering them by leaving the tap running. I know that school has taught them to do it and it's perfectly correct. I just find constantly having to turn the tap on really, really irritating.

And there's the television. I go into the lounge, flop down and grab the zapper. I have an urgent appointment with teletext page 325 (the League One table, what else?) or some other essential part of being a Father. What do I find? The children have turned the TV off to save power. It's not on standby, it's actually turned off. So I have to get up, walk to the telly and press the 'on' button. Now I know that shouldn't bother someone who remembers manually changing the channel. ("You can't have, Dad, that is like, so primitive…"), but it does, and – no surprise here – I find that really irritating as well.

Foolishly I made my feelings known the other night. The children were having a bit of a moan about my unreasonable behaviour – I'd made them eat their dinner – so I pointed out that sometimes I found their behaviour a tad irritating as well. The ringleader – Jessica, who else – soon organised a protest committee, and they were back with their revenge in about ten minutes. In they came with a list each: "5 Bad Things About Dad." It was like being pelted with rotten fruit.

- He leaves teletext on all the time
- He's prickly during the day 'cause he doesn't shave (be fair, Ben, only at the weekend)
- His cooking is awful – except spaghetti bolognese
- He makes stupid jokes
- He shouts too much (three votes for that one)
- He has a horrid singing voice (guilty as charged)
- He thinks he can do my homework

...And sundry others, over which I shall draw a discreet veil, as they're a) too personal, b) too disgusting – or both.

I studied the lists and then sent them away again. "Go on then," I said, "Five things that you like about your Dad."

"That's imposs-" Tom started and then remembered he wanted a new computer game. They were gone rather longer this time, but eventually they trooped back in.

Jessica immediately delivered a backhanded compliment. "He doesn't cook much," but at least she appreciated help with her homework. Tom chipped in with a vote for his Dad making him laugh, but Ben landed me in serious trouble. By this time Jane was reading over my shoulder and when she saw, "He gives me lots of sweets for no reason," she wasn't best impressed. While I was in the mood for self-analysis I briefly considered asking Jane to make two lists. But on balance it didn't seem a risk worth taking – especially when my score on her 'Urgent-Jobs-For-This-Weekend' list was a resounding nil.

No, the children seemed to have summed me up quite accurately. Someone who cooks spag bol and claims it as 50% of the housework, who can do year five Maths but who's starting to struggle with year six, and who divides his time between teletext and bribing the children with sweets. What's that about a role model...

Bedroom Farce

Ben came into the bedroom last night. Midnight – exactly. "I can't sleep, Daddy."

I could, but since when did that matter? "Just go back to your bedroom, try and think of something nice."

"There's a funny noise in my bedroom."

I sighed. Here we go again, I thought. Last week Jessica had been ill, she'd climbed in with Jane, and I'd been shuffled off to her room. Half an hour later Tom had a nightmare and didn't want to be alone on the top floor – so he kicked me out of Jessica's bed and I trudged up to the attic. At four o'clock it was Ben's turn to dream about vampires. (What had they eaten? Cheese Pie in cheese sauce?). So he had to get in with me. Of course, Mr. Wriggle forced me out of bed in about ten minutes flat, so while he slept contentedly I found myself downstairs, drinking tea and watching Underwater Truck Racing.

Why didn't I sleep in Ben's bed? After all, it would have completed the full set. Because you have to climb a ladder to get into Ben's bed, and I'm not sure it's safe – not for me anyway. But last night I was prepared to risk it. I was exhausted, it was too early for the sofa – and, besides, the Mongolian Superbike Championship wasn't on for another two hours.

I put a tentative foot on the ladder – sure enough, it started moving. Perhaps those last two screws that I'd abandoned when the football came on had been important after all. I'd considered this bed one of my better pieces of household engineering – only two days to build it and one solitary explosion of temper.

Now I had to climb off the ladder and into the bed. If there's nothing on TV and your child has this type of bed why not give it a try? Just make sure you've the osteopath's number handy.

Finally I made it – and stretched out hesitantly. The bed creaked and groaned ominously. There was a lesson here – never sleep on any piece of furniture I'd made myself. I expected the slats to give way at any moment. With any luck the noise of me crashing to the bedroom floor would wake Jane up. I was going to need her. If manoeuvering myself into the bed hadn't done for my back, landing on Ben's giant dumper truck most certainly would. As far as I could remember, the nice Swedish people we'd bought the bed off hadn't put any weight restrictions on the box – then again, maybe they'd assumed that anyone buying a child's bed wouldn't be daft enough to put an XL Dad into it.

I lay there feeling inadequate. I'd spent the evening watching Ray Mears build a canoe from birch bark and cedar, fasten it together with spruce roots and make it watertight with pine resin. Ben's bed had come in a box with idiot proof instructions. There wasn't much doubt which would last longer. More and more restless, my thoughts drifted back to the homework Tom had been doing at the weekend. It was a project on the

Second World War – all about smiling children being evacuated and resolute fathers building Anderson shelters.

"It's a good job there isn't a war on now isn't it, Dad?" he'd said. "Our family would be dead in ten minutes if you had to build the shelter."

Jessica had nodded. "The children would have to do it," she'd said. "With a bit of help from Mum." Then she'd given the knife a final twist. "You know, now we're older we don't really need Dad any more…"

Crime and Punishment

Tom is doing his homework. Across the room, Ben's on the computer. They're keeping up a running battle. "Tom's stupid," "Ben's a fat loser." You've heard it all before. I'm making a cup of tea and I'm just too tired to go and sort it out. They both shout at me to come and tell the other one off, but…who cares?

Then there's a noise. "Dad," Ben yells, "Come quick. Tom's broken the computer." This time, I go. It's not the computer, it's the screen. My lovely, almost brand new, £150 flat screen. The top third is fine – apart from the multi-coloured stripes. Below this there are bands of turquoise and black. And then there's a space-time vortex – exactly like the one the Tardis plunges through every Saturday night. And right at the centre of the vortex is a dent – a big one.

Sometimes you're so cross that you can't even lose your temper. "What happened?" I sigh.

"Tom threw a ruler at me, and it hit the computer."

Tom makes a half hearted denial and tries to blame Ben for ducking, but the evidence of the vortex is undeniable. The dent is fairly persuasive as well. "Why don't you claim on the warranty?" Tom asked later. Jane had to point out that it didn't cover an eleven year old boy hurling a twelve inch ruler at the screen.

So what's a suitable punishment? We've decided that they're both equally guilty, and they're banned from the computer for a month. Plus they can't have anything – toys, sweets, sports stuff, whatever they might want – until I've got my £150 back.

I stared bleakly into the vortex. Prayer seemed the only option. "Dad…" Tom started hesitantly.

"What now?"

"I know I can't have anything, but…can I still have my hair cut?"

For the next week I told my story of the shattered screen to any parent that would listen. It seemed to make several of them feel a good deal better about their own children. Friends countered with similar stories of misdeeds and retribution. Football through the lounge window (£50) – grounded for two weeks. Smashed the glass in front door panel in fit of temper (£117) – escaped punishment as child rushed to A&E with badly cut arm. Tom still held the record until I came to Lydia's Mum. "This'll cheer you up," I said.

"Nothing can cheer me up," she said sadly.

"Why not?" I tried to seem sympathetic, but this looked distinctly promising.

"We had the phone bill last week. £350. All down to Lydia…"

Suddenly all Tom's calls to Ollie to discuss computer games weren't so serious.

"…She'd been phoning her cousin in Australia."

"What did you do?"

Lydia's Mum reeled off a list of draconian punishments. As far as I could tell the poor child wouldn't be allowed out again until she was about

28. But will it work? Does any punishment work?

I broke my fair share of windows playing for England in the front garden. OK, I never racked up the phone bill like Lydia, but when we first had a phone you had to ask the operator if you wanted to ring next door. So if technology means that I can write this column sitting on a Greek beach and then e-mail it from an internet café (in my dreams – mind you, I did once e-mail it from Carlisle), then maybe we have to accept that it also means there's a £150 screen waiting for Tom's flying ruler. Perhaps it's time for some new instructions. "Don't argue, you two – but if you have to argue, remember not to duck..."

Total Embarrassment

Tom and I were in Karen's on Saturday getting our hair cut. Jessica was there as well. We were going into town afterwards and she was determined to stiff me for a new pair of trainers, and anything else her charming smile could extort. I was chatting, Karen was trying to cut out the grey hair and Tom was reading a magazine full of cars I'll never be able to afford. Jessica was bored.

Then one of the boys from her class came in. I'd spoken to him a few times so not unnaturally I said, "Hi, Luke." He stared back at me as though I was an alien. But that was nothing to the glare I received from Jessica.

"Dad," she hissed, "Be quiet."

"I only said 'hello'."

"You're embarrassing me."

"How can I embarrass you by saying 'hello'?"

She didn't reply. She fixed me with her steely eyes and dared me to open my mouth. I was strongly tempted to kiss her to see the reaction – but there were a lot of sharp objects lying around and Jessica looked like she wouldn't hesitate to use them. Naturally she gave me both barrels on the way to the sports shop.

"How could you embarrass me like that? By

speaking to him?"

"That's not embarrassing…"

"Don't you ever do it again." So now I had to take a vow of silence for the next nine or ten years – turn myself into a Trappist monk who just happens to drive a children's taxi and carry a credit card.

When we arrived home I asked Jessica what else I did that embarrassed her. "OK, Dad," she said, "But I'll need a big sheet of paper." In the end she managed to contain herself to five:

- Talking to her friends (see above)
- Buying clothes
- Trying to kiss her in front of other people
- Telling her off in public
- Talking about her

"So what about your Mum?" I said. "She's nowhere near as cool as me." Irritatingly Jane only scored two.

Determined to get a good report from somewhere I stalked off and asked Tom the same question. He didn't even bother looking up. "Singing and telling stupid jokes."

I turned to the internet for solace and typed "embarrassing parents" into the search engine. Google produced just the 345,000 responses. One report named the area of the country with the most embarrassing parents. Guess what? The North East. And you thought you looked pretty neat wandering round the Metro Centre…

In case you've read my list of failings and you're feeling rather smug at this stage, parents – especially Mums – can also mortify their children by 'behaving like a pop star.' Uncool food (soggy sandwiches and bland biscuits) in lunchboxes is also a big no-no, so next time you're wandering round Tesco remember to look for the 'Cool Food' aisle.

For Dads it boils down to three simple rules: don't speak, let your daughter choose your clothes and drive a Ferrari.

But you want really embarrassing parents? Go to America – the country where they're so bad they have their own Reality TV show. So, (according to the blurb), 'If your Mom dresses skimpier than Britney or your Dad keeps picking his nose' send the tape to PO Box 2500, Hollywood. Be sure to write 'Embarrassing Parents' on the package – as if they're going to mistake it for anything else. Like all American shows it's bound to be on our screens before long, so you might see me completely humiliating my daughter one night by doing something totally gross – like speaking to someone I know…

Gardener's Whirl

Heaven help me, the wretched woman I'm married to has decided we're going to build a patio. I'm the man who broke his toe tripping over some flat pack furniture – now I'm supposed to be auditioning for *Ground Force*.

I've always enjoyed the gardening programmes that Jane watches so avidly – they're a perfect opportunity to sneak away to the internet and see what price 'Pools are for tomorrow's game. Alas, Jane has seen one makeover too many. "I'd like to discuss the new patio with you," she said the other day. When a woman says that you know your peaceful weekends are set to become a dim and distant memory.

Jane's got her eye on a secluded – and long neglected – patch of concrete at the bottom of the garden. Supposedly it's all that remains of an ancient air raid shelter, although I can't see that bombing our house would have been a pivotal moment in World War 2.

You won't be surprised to hear that I like it the way it is. I sit there surrounded by a punctured football, a discarded plastic cutlass and a sunbathing cat and drink my beer in peace. Occasionally it does cross my mind that I'm in the ideal place for a patio, but what with summer going so quickly and the kids demanding so much attention…it's probably best to have another beer.

But Jane has signed the Compulsory Disturbance Order. We're going to have a patio, and it's going to be a family effort. Astonishingly, the kids have pitched in with gusto. Tom is digging – even to the exclusion of the computer. Jane asked him to level off the soil around the concrete and now we can't stop him – there's another genetic trait he didn't inherit from his Father. Ben is doing a sterling job as general 'tidier-upperer.' Jessica? You won't be surprised to hear that she's the self-appointed design co-ordinator. She now oversees the work clutching a paving catalogue, while mischievously suggesting octagonal designs that would give Tommy and Mr. Titchmarsh nightmares.

I'm in charge of levelling the concrete – specifically the odd square metre that's about three inches too high. I borrow a lethal looking metal stake from a friend who's clearly troubled by vampires and chip away for two hours – with absolutely no result. Eventually I put my sensible head on and present myself at the tool hire shop.

"You need an electric breaker, mate."

Right…apparently it's the children's version of a pneumatic drill.

Children's version or not, when it's produced from the back of the shop it still looks mightily impressive to me. "Have you got a tranny for that?" Mr. Tool Hire asks. "It runs on a one-ten current." Do I look like the sort of man who has a transformer? I don't even know where my Philips screwdriver is. He takes pity on me. "OK, I'll chuck a tranny in for you."

'Chuck?' he must be joking. It might be the size of a car battery but it weighs as much as Tom and Ben combined. I can only assume there's a black hole at the centre of it.

I stumble to the car with drill in one hand and lead weight transformer in the other. You'd say that next week was looking fairly promising for the Hartlepool chiropractic industry.

But less than an hour later I'm surveying what could definitely pass for the level base of our patio – job done by the family working together. We celebrate in the only way possible – with a giant vat of ice cream and a trip to the builders' merchants to look at paving slabs...

Get Buster

Bullying is one of the curses of modern life isn't it? The way it makes the victim feel powerless, lowers their sense of self-worth, and generally makes their life a misery. People say, "Stand up to the bully." But what if the bully is twice your size, three times as aggressive and covered in black and white fur?

Make no mistake about it, our cat is being bullied. There's Yikes, happily settling down to his delicious chicken flavour (with rabbit bites on top, no less) when in through the cat flap comes rough, tough Buster from three doors away.

Generally speaking I like animals – except Buster. He's rude, he's vicious and the pattern of the fur round his head makes him look suspiciously like a hoodie.

So what are we going to do about it? I can't exactly march down the road and demand they control their cat. Even Jessica doesn't see that as a practical solution – besides, the husband is about seven feet tall. We'll have to sort Buster out ourselves. Covert ops, here we come.

I marched into the supermarket and thought I'd bought the solution for £1.98 – twin water pistols at dawn. "Just wait," I said to myself. "When Buster comes through that cat flap Tom and I will be lying in ambush." I was still congratulating myself when I went to the bank and put my lethal weapons down on the counter. You could feel the man watching the CCTV getting ready to push the panic button.

"What's the water pistol for?" the woman behind the counter asked. I told her. She suggested pepper (actually she suggested an appointment with their financial adviser, but pepper was her second idea.)

I know that's supposed to work but how do you avoid peppering your own cat? Worse still, how do you avoid peppering your children? That would make for an interesting discussion with social services.

Besides, I might not like Buster but I don't want to do that – after all, there is the size of my neighbour to think about... No, the water pistols were definitely the answer – until Jessica discovered them.

"Daddy," she said, marching in to see me and holding a water pistol distastefully between her thumb and forefinger, "I've found this – can you tell me what it's for?"

"Oh, nothing, darling..."

"Daddy, you have always told us how important it is to tell the truth. Is it anything to do with Buster?" There was no option – I 'fessed up. Jessica was appalled.

"That is the most awful thing I have ever heard. Cats don't like water."

"That's the general idea."

"Well, it's definitely illegal. Supposing the police found out?" I was more worried about our neighbour finding out. That seemed much more likely – especially if St. Jessica suddenly appeared on the doorstep asking about Buster's health.

"So what do you suggest?" I asked.

"Well," Jessica began, "Mummy and I have been talking…" That sounded expensive. It was – between them they'd decided that a radio controlled collar was the answer. I pointed out that Yikes could lose it in the garden and be locked out.

"That's why you need to give me enough for two collars," Jessica explained with a sigh and an outstretched palm.

"What's he going to do then? Hide the spare in the garden and remember to get changed if he loses the first one?"

I should know by now that sarcasm isn't the weapon to use on my daughter. You may think your children can slam the door – not as hard as Jessica they can't. Anyway, Jane and Jessica are now in town buying a radio-controlled cat collar. There's another argument I've lost – maybe I could sabotage it with my water pistol and ask the shop for refund…

Visiting Time

My Mum was taken into hospital two weeks ago. She lay there, one tube supplying oxygen, another measuring the output from her failing kidneys. As the children have grown older they've learned more about Granny's blood pressure, and the problems it might cause one day. Now I was having to answer their "What if…" questions, and wonder when Mum might be well enough to see them.

I was in two minds about that. If the worst happened I didn't want their last memory to be of a frail old lady, surrounded by tubes. But I avoided the same memory about my own Gran when I was fourteen – and I've regretted it ever since.

So we took them – although Tom was reluctant at first. "I don't want to go," he said.

"Why not?"

"In case she's worse."

But she wasn't – after a week she was on the mend. Never mind what the doctors said, she suddenly ate a double portion of NHS liver and onions. What other sign of recovery do you need? We'll still be visiting for a while yet, but the atmosphere's a lot lighter – especially when I take Jessica. She abandons me in the car park, bounds through the maze of corridors, and when I pant up the stairs five minutes later she's sitting happily on her Gran's bed, studying the latest blood pressure chart.

As we walked back to the car she asked me about Heaven. "Do you believe in it?" I said.

"No."

"God?"

"Definitely not." That seemed like an awful lot of school assemblies going to waste. "It's silly," she said, "The idea of a man in a cloud looking after everything."

"So what happens after you die?"

She thought for a moment. "I think you come back as an animal – depending on what sort of person you've been."

"Right…"

"The best ones are lions, cheetahs and elephants," she said confidently. "I think Gran will be a cheetah. Because she was good at PE – when she was younger, I mean – and she was clever."

Like a fool I asked the obvious question. "What about me? What will I come back as?"

"A hip – " Wisely, she thought better of it. "I'm not sure, Daddy. Besides – " she said, changing the subject almost as expertly as Jane, "You didn't Spirigel. I'm telling…"

If you've been into a hospital ward lately you'll be familiar with Spirigel. It's the disinfectant that you squirt on to your hands as you walk in. Rub your hands together and they're magically clean and dry in thirty seconds. Better still, it's magnificently gooey, so the children love it. Whether they'll love the latest NHS suggestion – that we all have a bath or a shower before we go visiting – I'm not so sure. Wouldn't that mean 95% of children can only go on Sunday nights?

So far I've only taken one child at a time to visit Mum. Last night I risked it and took Tom and Jessica together. Needless to say by the time we left the ward they were arguing – and I could barely believe why.

"Well I washed my hands better than you did."

"No you did not, I used half a bottle."

"Only because it was the first time you washed your hands all week."

"Liar. Granny said I had the cleanest hands…"

Tom and Jessica, obsessed with washing their hands… Does that make me a successful parent? Or a complete failure, because I haven't managed in ten years what the NHS achieved in one week? Or does it just prove that whatever the circumstances, your kids will find something to argue about…

Indecent Exposure

That's another job crossed off my list – new passport photos for the boys. Mind you, I'm not sure why it was there in the first place because we're going to Derbyshire this year. Maybe Jane's had some divine intervention on our lottery numbers that she hasn't told me about.

Anyway, the photos are done, and at £3.50 each they're not bad at all – significantly better than the far more expensive (oh, and by the way, would you mind paying in advance?) school photos. There they are, two handsome boys, beaming back at me from their little squares.

By a curious coincidence the machine that produced these excellent pictures is the very one that promised to take a passport photo of me last year – and instead produced one of an overweight middle aged person with a double chin and distinct signs of grey hair. They've obviously had it fixed in the last twelve months.

The trouble is, the boys' passport photos probably won't be acceptable to HM Passport Service. Having filled in the forms, enclosed their old passports, persuaded Jane to write the cheque and put them in the post, I then read the instructions. Big Brother – the original one – would have been proud. You want an acceptable passport photo? It's easy – don't smile, don't wear a hat, don't get too close – or too far away, don't look sideways…the list goes on. I fell heavily at the first hurdle.

So will the applications come back to us? Or will we only find out that we've failed to match these wretched guidelines – from the International Civil Aviation Organisation no less – when we reach a Greek arrivals desk one day?

A wake up call is needed here. By definition we don't need our passports for the short trip to Derbyshire, when we may well arrive looking more or less normal. No, if we're using our passports, four factors automatically apply:

- We're landing somewhere hot
- We're travelling as a family
- We've spent several hours on a crowded plane
- Before that we were at the airport for what seemed like three days, and relations are – to put it mildly – slightly strained

Therefore my children now bear absolutely no resemblance to the ones who had their photos taken on Sunday morning, having just been ordered to comb their hair and make the acquaintance of a face-cloth. With due respect to the ICAO, may I suggest that if they want any hint of realism children's passport photos should show the following:

- An embryonic black eye (thanks to a brotherly punch-up somewhere over France)
- A mouth ringed with chocolate (Excellent – you

didn't give in until the pilot said, "We are now crossing the English Channel…")

- A chin and T-shirt covered in sick. (The airline may have thought it was a 'delicious satay sauce' but your child didn't. Not after that turbulence).

Obviously if your children are teenagers then these points don't apply, but for total authenticity the passport photo should show two things – an iPod surgically attached to one ear and a mobile phone glued to the other.

And what holds good for children also applies to their parents. Far from the bland expression demanded by the obviously-childless men at the ICAO, your passport photo should show a mixture of emotions. Wonder – should I have married that ex-girlfriend who said she never wanted children? Worry – if the holiday continues like this the words 'solicitor' and 'divorce' could feature strongly on our return. And of course, complete exhaustion – and while the photo-booth is dealing with that little lot, maybe it could do something about your double chin as well…

Seven Deadly Sins

I was talking to a friend of mine the other day – or rather he was talking and I was having a visit from the green-eyed monster. "It was our anniversary last week," he said. "We went to Florence."

"Lovely," I said, through gritted teeth. It was our anniversary the other week as well. We went to Tesco's.

"While we were there Hazel decided we needed a new kitchen." Did she? Jane frequently decides we need a new kitchen – even more frequently she decides we need a new house, but something seems to stop us. It's called a cash flow – specifically cash flowing to the children, and trickling to us. As you may have guessed, my friend and his wife don't have children.

And then what does he say to me? "I tell you – life's stressful at the moment." Stressful? Does he know what the word means? His GP should write him a simple prescription. "Three children, to be taken to school, dropped off at football, netball and sundry other sports, kept off the computer, fed, watered and clothed…" You get the drift – if the NHS wants to contact me, I'm sure we could make our three available every so often. Then Jane and I could watch a TV programme about Florence and wonder why we weren't there.

Well, that's better – sorry if I've gone off the deep end. It's Jessica's fault, she's been doing a school project on the seven deadly sins. Needless to say I've been subject to a relentless barrage of cross-examination, and I'm not sure that I came out of it very well. She seemed to place a tick under rather too many columns.

"Sloth, Dad. What's that?" she started.

"Being lazy," I replied. "Something you definitely can't accuse me of."

"Tick," she said. "Far too much time spent watching football, and Mum says we have to hide the remote before England play Australia."

She checked off Gluttony without too much trouble, didn't even bother to discuss Anger, and was just moving on to Pride when Jane walked in. "Jessica, your bedroom is a disgrace."

I smirked in triumph. "Got you," I said to Jessica. "What's that then, sweetheart? Sloth?"

"Gluttony," said Jane, "Judging by the number of sweet wrappers I've found stuffed behind her bed."

While Jessica shot upstairs to try and hide the evidence, I casually ticked off the sins of my children. Untidy bedrooms, not eating fruit and veg – it was going to be too easy. Sloth? That was simply the length of time it took Tom to come off the computer.

Tom's winding me up over another one as well. I'm having a bit of a thing about 'please' and 'thank you' at the moment. Tom's twelve fairly soon and he's started drifting towards that special teenage language that consists entirely of grunts and stamping your foot.

I would like to hear the words just once more, before he disappears completely into the teenage abyss. I bought him a pair of sunglasses last week and did he say anything? No chance. Alright, strictly speaking, they were on 'buy one get one free' and I'd bought myself a pair, but you know what I mean. Otherwise the next time I hear 'please' will be when he wants the deposit on a house.

I was starting to make myself quite grumpy when Jessica re-appeared. She was sweetness and light and back on the subject of sin. "There's one on this list we didn't do at school, Dad…"

"What's that?"

"Lust," she said. "What does it mean?"

"I can't remember," I said. "It's something you find in Florence, I think…"

Harry Potter and the Reign of Terror

A despot has taken over our house. Queen Jessica the Merciless is now in charge. She is blackmailing her brothers and her parents. As soon as she opens her mouth to speak I offer her chocolate to keep quiet. Last time I saw Jane she was discussing a bedroom makeover with her. Tom has even stopped fighting with Her Majesty. Fortunately for our sanity, the evil empire won't last much beyond next weekend – by that time we'll all have finished the new Harry Potter.

I had to be in Newcastle early last Saturday. I rang home to speak to the kids at around eight. "They won't come to the phone," Jane said.

"What do you mean they won't come to the phone?"

"They're reading. Harry Potter has arrived."

"What about Ben? He can't read that well."

"The others won't come so he won't come. Sorry – bye."

I came back to an eerily quiet house. Thanks to Jane's credit card – and a postman who must have wanted the weekend off – two copies of *The Half Blood Prince* had arrived at seven in the morning. Tom and Jessica were nowhere to be seen. Vague sounds of playing came from Ben's bedroom, but otherwise the house was deserted. "I'm home," I shouted. There was no reply.

"I'm back..." Still no reply.

"Does anyone want a sandwich?" There was more life on the *Marie Celeste*.

"Hello," I shouted, "I've been to a chocolate factory..."

Eventually Jane wandered in from the garden. "Jessica's already on page 110," she said. "We'll never catch her up."

But why worry? Because from then on Jane and I had a blissful weekend. We read the Sunday papers, sorted out a big chunk of the garden, drank red wine at lunchtime and generally chilled out. There were no punch-ups, no demands to be taken anywhere, no shouts of "It's not fair," just the gentle murmur of me repeating, "It can't last much longer..."

It couldn't, of course. On Monday afternoon Jane was supposed to collect Jessica from school. She came into the house alone. "Where's Jessica?" I asked.

"She's in the car – sixty pages to go. Says she's staying there until she's finished it."

And she did. Jessica finally came in at quarter to seven, blinking as she slowly returned to normal life.

"Do you want some tea?" I asked.

"I can't believe it," Jessica replied.

"Can't believe what?"

"Who died in Harry Potter. The last person I expected..."

"I don't want to know."

"You won't believe it…"

"You're right, I won't, because you're not going to tell me."

Gradually a look of realisation dawned on her face, quickly followed by one of sly cunning. "I think I'll just have sweets for tea, Dad," she said.

"In your dreams. And don't forget you need to tidy your bedroom."

She looked at me shrewdly. "It's quite amazing who died. Are you sure, Dad…"

Since then we have lived under a reign of terror. That was all Tony Blair needed to do to get his own way at the G8 summit – get himself an advance copy and threaten to tell George Bush the ending. Then he could have spent his time playing on the computer, eating chocolate and not tidying his bedroom. Jane and I are going as fast as we can, but I don't think we'll be released from the tyranny until Sunday night.

Meanwhile Jessica's power increases as news filters round her friends that she's finished the book. I even saw the Headmaster looking at her nervously this morning – I suspect her report could be quite good this term…

Father of the Man?

So let's see what Mr. Teale had to say about me as an eight year old…"Rather keen on football – perhaps a little too much at times." No change there then – what about the rest of it? I seem to have been a conscientious little boy – until we reach Crafts that is. "Shows no interest whatsoever." Perhaps Jane should have looked at my school reports before she married me, then she wouldn't have spent so many years asking me to put shelves up…

I stumbled across the old reports last week – at the risk of shattering the rosy impression I had of my academic progress, I read them all. Primary school was much as I remembered it, but secondary school? Not quite. I was fairly sure the reports from my teenage years were good (on the whole) with the just the occasional lapse. No – they painted a fairly dismal picture of the wheels gradually falling off.

Could do Better? I wish they'd been so kind. At least old Beaky eventually had the courage to write honestly. "Lazy. If he gave one-tenth of the attention to Chemistry that he gives to football and girls he would do well. He doesn't. He won't." He was right though – you could put my school reports in a row and see exactly when the words 'Angela Miller' became significant in my life.

If I'm honest I still try and get by with the minimum of effort, I'm still too interested in football, and the world knows I'll never be any good at 'Crafts.' So on Friday night I opened the children's school reports with a shaking hand – was this going to be another case of the child being the father of the man?

I decided to start with Ben and work upwards. "I have enjoyed being with Ben this year," Mrs. Smith had written. It looked like this one could cost me money. He was mixing well with everyone – but "He must guard against talking too much." Hmm…we've never had a politician in the family.

Previous readings of this column may have given you the view that Jessica is opinionated and a trifle bossy. Not at school, where she transforms into 'Bunty of Mallory Towers' – whatever activity is going, Jessica will do it. But, like her Dad, she draws the line at Design Technology (which I gather is 'Crafts' in new money). The teacher made a valiant effort – he finished with "She is a pleasure to teach." What he really meant was "She's not interested but she gives me that charming smile and I'm putty in her hands." Join the club, mate.

Tom, I learned, was "Quiet, hard working and well motivated." They've obviously never asked him to set the table. To no-one's surprise he'd made "Excellent progress in all areas of ITC." Whether it will say the same in a couple of years when he's hacked into the secondary school mainframe remains to be seen.

With a severe jolt I realised that both Tom and Jessica had scored top marks in the PHSE exam – which I'm fairly sure is something to do with personal health and moral education. This is quite astonishing given that we have to nag them ceaselessly to clean their teeth, and (despite Jane's warnings) I constantly leave the internet on the page displaying the best price for 'Pools this season. (18/1 if you're interested).

My own exam results weren't quite so spectacular – especially History, when I found myself sitting next to a sun-kissed Angela. Did she really need to wear such a short skirt for an exam? I certainly spent the three hours concentrating furiously, but not on Bismarck's foreign policy...

Xbox Blues

So here I am on the internet, poised to pay Amazon thirty quid for a product I neither want nor understand. As I don't want it but I'm still buying it then you might guess that it's for the children. As I don't understand it, you might also guess that it's something to do with computers and it's probably for Tom. Right on all three counts.

I am buying an "Xbox Live starter kit". Tom has vaguely explained what it does – more to the point he's nagged ceaselessly, day and night, until Jane and I have finally buckled under the strain and given in.

Three hours ago I nearly bought it for £14.99, thanks to the on-the-hour-online sale some computer shop was having. Unfortunately, by the time I'd given them my Mother's maiden name, the first school I attended, the first girl I kissed and the order in which I cut my toenails, it was too late. All 50 they had at £14.99 were gone. We waited patiently for another hour (a driving game) – and another hour (a vibrating steering wheel, presumably for those three hundred word a minute typists who managed to buy the driving game). Faced with the choice of spending the next ten hours by the computer hoping that the Xbox special offer would be repeated (it wasn't – I checked on Monday) or coughing up the extra money to boost

Amazon's profits and give myself some peace for the weekend, I naturally surrendered.

Two days on I vaguely remember that Tom sold it to us on the grounds of "teamwork" – as though the Xbox is the modern equivalent of the Boy Scouts. And there was something about "making friends in different countries," as well. Given that the only sounds we've heard since it arrived are "Good kill," "Cover me," and "Get the sniper," global harmony seems a little way off at the moment.

Mind you, I find it quite mind-boggling that he can sit in our lounge, play against someone in Hong Kong and simultaneously speak to them via a headset. It certainly puts the twenty minutes I spent trying to get through to a call centre in Newcastle into perspective.

I'd quite like a game myself, but there's no chance – Tom won't let me play because I would be shot repeatedly and thrashed into last place. Touching, I hear you say, he doesn't want his Dad to be embarrassed. Huh – the truth is that like some global sales manager Xbox mercilessly tracks your statistics – number of games played, finishing position, number of times you were snipered – all that wholesome stuff.

If I played I'd ruin Tom's figures and expose him to ridicule when his friends came round.

"So let's see your stats, Tom."

"My Dad played some of those games, honest."

"Yeah, right – loser."

So the world will be spared my one tactic for any shoot-'em-up game. As I'm too old to work the controls properly I simply spin continuously through 360 degrees, firing constantly. Tom howls with derision and contempt, but I do occasionally shoot someone – although they're usually on my side. This explains my standard score of minus twenty and Tom's decision to ban me.

Meanwhile I sit back and mourn the passing of the TV, too exhausted from the weekend to nag him to come off – and I was quite looking forward to watching the next Test Match. I could go on the computer instead, but Ben is busy dropping nuclear bombs on Russia. He should be ready for the Xbox just as Tom gives it up for girls. Looks like my ban could be a long one...

Ain't No Cure...

I had a day off last Thursday. The sun was shining, the birds were singing and Trescothick and Strauss were thumping the Aussies to every corner of Edgbaston. If only I'd been watching them... Instead I was in the garden, refereeing a small altercation between my children. And then I had to entertain them.

The summer holidays are proving something of a problem this year. We've always had my Mum to rely on in the past – she's out of hospital now, but the days of Gran having one of the children won't be coming back. So Jane and I are blundering through, juggling annual leave, childminders, football courses and prayer in an attempt to make it to September – and vainly hoping to keep our sanity, our jobs and our overdraft under some sort of control.

At the moment it's a losing battle. I feel like a cartoon character – you know the one, desperately hanging on with his fingernails, but starting to slide faster and faster down the side of the building. Still, I'll get used to it – the only way we can cope is if I take every Thursday off until the end of August.

My mood wasn't improved when I opened the paper and found that the national cost of looking after your kids through the summer holidays was £9 billion.

"Parents count the cost of holidays," the article was headed. "Parents hide behind sofa when credit card statement arrives," you mean.

You won't be surprised to hear that the main area for spending is the South East, where some parents splash out the equivalent of a 'Pools season ticket every week. Well, sending the children to the Ritz for their tea every day does mount up a bit, I suppose. On the other hand, after the Bradford game...

The same article advises me that not only should I have a special savings account to pay for the summer holidays (that's assuming you didn't raid it in February for clothes or food), but that I should also keep my children amused with "mini-workshops", such as chocolate making sessions, and painting their own designs on T-shirts.

There are two small points here. Number one – England have Australia by the throat, which may never happen again in my lifetime. To put it mildly, I am unlikely to pass it up for a chocolate making session. Number two, there is no doubt whatsoever that these articles are written by journalists with no children and trendy wooden floors that wipe clean in an instant. I can just imagine the conversation I'd have with Jane as she opened the door after one of the recommended sessions.

"So what have you done with the children today, dear?"

"We made chocolate and then I encouraged them to paint their own clothes. Perhaps I'll go and live in Argentina for a while..."

Still, I'd be in Persil's good books. They've just

announced – after years of research, apparently – that spending the summer holidays getting dirty is positively good for children. That's along the lines of the instructions on the back of the milk-shake powder the children are currently addicted to: "For best results use four heaped teaspoons." One is perfectly adequate, thank you, unless you want to move in with your dentist. And I'm grateful for the advice, Persil, but on balance I'd prefer to keep my marriage intact.

At least the children are a joint problem for the next seven days. We're off to a cottage in the Derbyshire Peaks. Mercifully, the long range weather forecast looks good. You know what they say – it's better to travel hopefully...

God Bless

The first two days of our holiday in Derbyshire were perfect – blue sky, well behaved children, cold beer and a good book. Then, at ten past five on Monday evening, my mobile phone rang.

It was my brother. "We think Mum's had a stroke," he said. He tried to tell me not to do anything until the GP had called, but I was already reaching for the car keys. First, though, I had to tell the children.

"Tom," I yelled into the garden, "Jessica, Ben."

"What do you want?" They were damming up a stream – whatever I wanted, it couldn't be that vital.

"I need to talk to you. It's important – really important."

I hugged them as fiercely as I could, and climbed into the car. Two hours and fifty minutes later I pulled up at the Hospice, still in my shorts. We'd once talked to her GP about Mum going in for some respite care – now it was the real thing. The consultant was explaining that it hadn't been a stroke, but it was still... I wasn't listening.

Mum smiled weakly at me. "Where are the children?" she asked.

"On holiday, Mum," I said. "With Jane. I've left them to come and see you."

"I'm sorry," she whispered. "I didn't want to spoil

your holiday."

I tried to tell her not to be silly, but I couldn't get the words out. I just held her and started to cry. I did that a lot over the next two days – and wondered where I should be. Half of me wanted to be with my children, comforting them. I knew that's what Mum would want me to do – but how could I leave?

By Tuesday night Mum was sleeping peacefully – the sedatives had finally done their work. I phoned Jane, told the children how much I loved them, and collapsed into bed. On Wednesday morning she was still asleep, breathing evenly and almost looking well. I kissed her, told her I loved her and that I'd see her on Friday, and went back to the children.

The phone rang as I was driving down the M1. I recognised the number, risked the fine and answered it. It was one of the nurses. "I'm so sorry…" she said. I sat in the car park at Woodall Services and tried to come to terms with it. We'd said everything to each other that we'd wanted to say. Mum had talked about seeing Dad again, she was at peace with herself and she wasn't frightened – what more could I ask?

Jane knew as soon as I got out of the car. "Where are they?" I asked.

"What do you think? They're building another dam…" So we walked down to the stream, and as gently as we could, told the children that their Gran had died.

And now tomorrow we have the funeral. When I can focus on the laptop through the tears I'm busy writing my speech. In the next room Tom is on the Xbox, and Jessica and Ben are chasing each other round the garden. No doubt there'll be an argument in the next five minutes. On the surface just another day in an ordinary family – except for our family, a large part of the foundations were taken away this week. I don't know how the children will react long term – but I know that when they walk into church tomorrow they'll make me proud.

And some time in the eulogy I'll look up and catch sight of Jessica, who has so much of her Gran in her. And I'll try to do what Mum would have wanted – love my children, and look forward, not back...

Family Viewing

Jessica has just marched in from the garden to tell me that Nathan is an "Extremely horrible little boy." I rather like Nathan – the real reason Jessica's so cross is that he's turned up at our house to play with Ben, while her friends are otherwise occupied.

For a child Nathan's a spectacularly good gossip. His family's moved house and now he tells me that according to his Mum they "Can't afford healthy food any more." She should look on the bright side. Ben – the human fruit blender – had a telling off from the dentist last week for eating too much of the stuff and needing a filling. So much for five units a day...

Obviously though, Jessica knows best. "Nathan said a swear word, Daddy. If I were you I wouldn't allow him in the house."

If I was making a list of friends I wouldn't allow in the house Nathan would be at the bottom. Some of Tom's might be rather closer to the top. Unlike Tom they all seem to be the youngest in their family – so they turn up with a good selection of DVD's and PS2 games stolen off their older brothers.

Lennie – not his real name, but his Dad used to be in the Marines – was a good example. He turned up with two DVD's – *Matrix* and *Family Guy*, both of which had 15 prominently displayed on the box. One of the games for the PS2 was a 12 – barely worth playing. The other was a wrestling game called *SmackDown versus Raw*.

"I haven't heard of that one," I said to Lennie. He looked at me with contempt – clearly it would have been a major shock if I had. They decided to watch *Family Guy*.

"What's it about?" I asked Tom.

"It's really cool. I've already seen it at Ollie's house."

I'm not sure that 'really cool' was the description I'd have chosen. The action seemed to centre on the family's dog, who in the two episodes I saw became addicted to drugs and started a career in the adult movie business. At that point I decided enough was enough and I'd deal with the protests later.

Am I being over-protective? I can still remember sneaking into an X – as if the cinema cared I now realise. It was a wet Tuesday in February and they needed the money. What did it matter to them if three 15 year olds who should have been in double Maths were creeping in to see the antics of a Swedish air hostess?

What worries me is that the Internet now serves up videos that are as different from the mild behaviour of the air hostess as I am from the men that appear in them. Will we have *Family Guy* this year and the seamier side of the Web next year? I strongly suspect that whatever we come up with in terms of Net Nanny or Cyberwatch, Tom will find a way round it in about three seconds. And if he doesn't, he'll simply go to a friend's house where they didn't have it in the first place.

And what about bad language? As I take my children to watch 'Pools occasionally – and sit behind the goal – why do I worry about it in films? After all, I let Ben finish off my bottles of beer – so why don't I start and introduce Tom to some mild pornography?

As usual I don't know the answer. Like most parents I'm just muddling through, doing the best I can. Thank goodness I've got Jessica to tell me what to do…

Home Cooking

So guess what's the latest craze in our house... The portable PS2? Some hideous game for Xbox Live that's giving me sleepless nights? No – it's baking.

Armed with the 1958 edition of the *Be-Ro Flour Book of Home Baking*, Jessica is churning out a regular supply of cakes, buns and biscuits. She visited Grandma last week and came back with a bulging bag of chocolate buns she'd helped to make. The next day some misdemeanour saw her receive a two day ban from sweets. Thirty minutes later she'd dodged that by giving Jane her best smile and asking if Mum would show her how to bake a cake. Now she stands in the kitchen, sleeves rolled up, ordering her faithful assistant, Tom, to sieve some cocoa powder.

Want your children to work happily together without any fighting? Throw away all those modern parenting theories and give them a 1950s recipe book... Actually I'm not sure that 'working together' is quite right – Jessica is very much in charge. If you're old enough to remember them from black and white TV, Fanny Craddock and Johnny have been re-born.

"Pass me some kitchen roll, Tom, and some margarine – quickly."

"I can't, I'm having a drink."

That wasn't the answer Fanny had been looking

for. "In that case I'll let Ben lick the bowl out. And I need some caster sugar…"

"Where is it?"

"In the cupboard," Jessica sighed – and gave him the patient look Jane gives me at similar moments.

"I still can't find it." The similarities were scary.

Jessica rolled her eyes theatrically and burrowed in the cupboard herself. She came out with a bedraggled looking packet with around three grains of caster sugar in it.

"Why don't you just use granulated?" I thought it was time I stuck my six pennyworth in.

"Mum says it makes the buns gritty."

What did I care? Any buns were long gone before I was allowed anywhere near them.

To her credit Jessica has jumped straight in at the deep end – no messing about in the 'children's cooking' section for her. The 'Sticky Blobs' and the 'Animal Biscuits' have received short shrift. The book now falls open at milk chocolate cake – which has an orange square next to it, meaning 'more involved baking'. If you're reading this, Jessica, I'll admit to a serious weakness for profiteroles with chocolate sauce – page 43, and they're an orange square as well.

Profiteroles aside – and you may find this hard to believe for a man that's fighting a losing battle to stay in a 36" waist – I'm not really that keen on chocolate cake and the like. I eat a small slice of birthday cake and then feel sick for several hours. But once she's baked, there's no escaping Jessica.

"I've brought you a slice of cake, Dad," she says, thrusting a plate in front of me.

Stupidly, I once asked if I could eat it later.

"We're having ours now, Dad," she said, an ominous edge creeping in to her voice.

"Please, Jessica, I'm a bit full." At that she rattled round the house for an hour wailing that I didn't love her and hated her cooking. Now I find the words, "Yum, I was just thinking about some cake," the safest option. Besides, what I don't eat the boys will soon hoover up.

Not that being Jessica's assistant has widened Tom's own cooking skills. Peanut butter sandwiches and tins of tomato soup remain the limit of his repertoire. I'll have to teach him to make Spag Bol. Then he'll be a fully qualified New Man – just like his Dad...

Warney The Second

Right now, this week's sporting hero is practising in the hall. Tom – or Shane as we must now learn to call him – is bowling leg breaks at the kitchen door. Needless to say his Mother is out.

I'm writing this column on Saturday morning – hopefully by the time you read it the nation's prayers will have produced the wettest three days on record and Michael Vaughan will be sleeping with the Ashes urn under his pillow. And if the enthusiasm for cricket running through Tom and his mates is any guide, the Aussies can forget about reclaiming it any time before 2050.

Mind you there is a down side – I was forced into the garden to bat at six-thirty this morning. Never mind appealing against the light, I tried to come off for a bacon sandwich. The main action takes place at tea time though, when I can persuade Jane to keep wicket for us.

Tom sets a pretty attacking field for his bowling – the garage door at silly point, Jane's best tub of plants in the slips, and what I think is a geranium at mid wicket. Unfortunately since we lost the ball in it that particular fielder is looking a bit trampled – well, crushed if the truth be told.

Much to Tom's frustration his Mother doesn't see

catching the ball as a central part of the wicket keeper's job. What's really important is shouting "Bowling, Tommy," and "Like it, Tom" after every ball. To add authenticity she does this in what she fondly thinks is an Australian accent. We need a wicky, so I won't tell her this, but it sounds more like she's spent a large part of her life in Ebbw Vale.

"I'm bowling a googly," Tom announces, showing me a grip that involves dislocating three fingers. He doesn't get the grip quite right as the ball pitches some distance outside off stump – in the neighbour's rose bed. The next one's a lot better. It's pitching just outside my leg stump. It'll spin and bounce too much so I could safely leave it, but I decide to look professional and pad it away. "Howwwzaaaatttt," Tom screams. Jane has seen too much of Billy Bowden and instantly raises a crooked finger.

"You can't give me out, you're the wicket keeper."

"I'm his Mum, of course I can give you out. Stop being a whinging Pom."

Three or four years ago I took Tom to the Scarborough Cricket Festival. "Can I get autographs, Dad?" he asked. I still bear the emotional scars of receiving a very short reply from Geoff Boycott when I pushed a scruffy piece of paper and a stubby pencil in front of him. I couldn't believe that today's cricketers were much different, but you can't protect your children from everything. Yorkshire were warming up when we arrived. The nearest player to us when practice finished was the future captain of England. "Go on then," I said to Tom. "Go and ask him."

What had I worried about? Vaughany signed his book with a smile – then he saw I'd a camera with me and offered to have his photo taken with Tom. Later that afternoon he was fielding on the boundary – about three yards from us. He spent five overs chatting to Tom like an old friend.

So there'll be a biblical flood, or heroics from Freddie Flintoff, or some outstanding batting – anything will do. And some time on Monday the nicest sportsman I've met will be clutching the Ashes urn – even if he is responsible for me missing my bacon sandwich and getting a dodgy lbw decision...

Football Crazy

"Not in the house, Jessica."

"But you told me to practise – I'll never be any good if I don't practise."

"Right, and that's why you should go out of the back door and into the garden."

"But it's dark."

"So you'll have to do it tomorrow, but in the meantime you can't kick your football up and down the stairs."

"Well, Dad, you don't know what you're talking about." And with that the future captain of the England women's football team flounces upstairs and slams her bedroom door.

Here I am with two boys and right now it's my daughter that's driving me mad kicking a ball about. Jessica has joined a girls under 12 team – they haven't played any matches yet, but my goodness do they take their training seriously. It was bucketing down the other Saturday. "Training won't be on," I said to Jessica.

"It might be. We'll have to go."

"Jessica, our garden is under water. You can't possibly train in this."

We went, of course. We didn't have a number for Dave the Coach but Jessica would have made me go anyway.

The rain had eased to torrential by the time we reached the school playing field. That would have been enough for me to decide to discuss tactics in the pub but it didn't deter Dave and the girls. There were six of them. Two Man Utd's, an Arsenal, a Newcastle Michael Owen (what else?) and a Real Madrid. Judging by the number of Spanish and Italian shirts you now see round town, buying one is as much a part of the holiday as fighting off the time share boys and girls. Jessica was in a red England top, red shorts and red socks – so Liverpool in all but sponsor's logo. "Why Liverpool?" I asked. For some reason they're the one team I've always disliked.

"They're my fourth favourite team," she said. I have to hold my hand up and say that's a major failure on the father's part – how can anyone have four favourite football teams? And how can the order go Man Utd, Arsenal, 'Pools, Liverpool? There's six games a year where you have hopelessly divided loyalties – more in the unlikely event of 'Pools going on a stunning cup run...

Back at the school the girls are warming up. I don't know what's on the FA coaching course at the moment – as far as I can see from what my kids do it consists largely of warming up and warming down. Personally I'd rather they learned to kick properly but what do I know? Jessica usually warms up by fighting her brothers in the car on the way to training. And as every child will tell you, there's no better warm down than eating a bar of chocolate...

A practice match finally gets under way. Jessica's a midfielder, and she's not bad. As they say in the game, she's 'got a good engine,' and can 'get from box to box' – or in this case, set of yellow cones to pile of jumpers. Factor in her ability to go ballistic and you've got a female Roy Keane.

As I dashed for the car Dave handed me the club's Parents Charter – based on the FA's guidelines apparently. There's all the stuff you'd expect, including one that says the result isn't important – and there was me getting upset about England losing 1-0 to Northern Ireland.

And of course, you've got to encourage your child as much as possible, and make sure they practise. So maybe Jessica's right after all. "That's a beautiful volley up the stairs, Jess, right into the plant pot. Now let's see what the Parents' Charter says about clearing up the mess before your mother gets home…"

Body Clocks

Regular readers will know that my daughter, Jessica, has always had the body clock of a university student. Number one son is clearly destined to be a farmer or a milkman. Which is fine – except that they live in the same house, and we're the parents.

Jessica was born at two o'clock in the morning. She came into the world with her eyes wide open, checking us out. "That's good," I stupidly thought, "Tom wakes up early as well so it'll be OK."

I now know that was complete rubbish. She was wide-eyed and alert because that was her natural time for being awake. I should have taken the hint at the time and started driving a late night taxi for practice.

Ever since then, Jessica's body clock has been a mystery to us. We have sent her to bed early, we have established a bedtime routine, we've read to her, we have sat on the floor, linked hands and chanted. Whatever we do, two things cannot be changed. She will not go to sleep before 10:00, and every evening around seven she goes mad for thirty minutes.

In desperation I asked my new best friend, Google, for help. In went the phrase, 'Body clock teenager,' and back came a glut of information – admittedly most of it based on a study of American teenagers in Sacramento.

Clearly too much knowledge for a parent is a dangerous thing. I'd always thought Jessica was simply in a bad temper, probably brought on by eating too many sweets when no-one was looking. Thanks to the internet I'm now informed that nothing could be more wrong. At seven o'clock she's having a circadian rhythm 'dip', caused by a part of her brain called the Suprachiasmatic Nucleus. Fancy not knowing that – goodness me, I'm hardly fit to be a father.

Back in Sacramento the learned studies say that the average American teenager is sleep deprived – unlike our house where it's the average parent. So if you thought your teenage child was just lazy – and like Jane's mother used to, you've perfected the art of changing the bed while there's a teenager still lying there – you'd be wrong.

It's biological. Something happens in teenagers' brains and they have to go to bed later and sleep later than adults – so Heaven help Jane and I in three years time. Ships that pass in the night? I'll be lucky if I see my wife awake more than once a month.

The American solution was to push back the start of school – and grades are improving and truancy is down. Mind you, they used to kick off at 7:15 in the morning. I don't think there's a number low enough to accurately reflect our chances of getting Jessica to school at 7:15 – even 8:45 is seriously optimistic.

In fact, if Jessica's headmaster is reading this, I'd like to let you know that she'll be in a little later from now on – say, elevenish? That way you can count on perfect behaviour, sparkling exam results and a stress-free father.

And yet despite all this there's an interesting paradox. Tom charges out of bed at around 6:15 in the morning. Some considerable time later Jessica is winched from the pit. But come school time, which one is them is perfectly dressed, teeth brushed, everything organised and generally ready for action? And which one is frantically stuffing kit into his PE bag, hunting for his books, trying to find his shoes and driving us mad? Is that just my children? Or at the risk of giving Jane some more ammunition, does it prove something fundamental about men and women...

Modern Art

Tom has started secondary school, and to be honest, I'm struggling with the homework. Not the Maths or the English – I can leave that to Tom. It's when he asks for help with Art that the fun begins.

Casting my mind back several decades I can't remember any such thing as Art homework, but it's clearly an integral part of modern schooling. "We have to show something re-arranged in a different way," Tom said on Sunday morning.

"That's no problem at all," I said. "Go and tidy your bedroom and take a photo of it."

Which is exactly the sort of stupid remark that sees Jessica slam the door so hard that she threatens the house insurance. Tom is more laid back. He just snarled at me and went off on his bike for half an hour.

I tried to be more diplomatic with my second attempt. "You need to re-arrange something?"

"Yes."

"Have you got anything in mind?"

"No."

I wracked my brains. "Paper? You could tear some paper up…" Tom looked at me with contempt.

"Why don't you make some buns?" Jessica suggested hopefully. "That way you've re-arranged flour and chocolate powder."

Even I could see that it wouldn't do Tom's credibility any good to wander into school with a plate of fairy cakes.

"Why don't I break a mug and then stick it back together?" Well, it certainly made a change for one of my boys to actually think about breaking something before they did it. I was about to tell Tom it was out of the question when Jane said, "OK, I saw an old mug at the back of the cupboard." There's a lesson in that – Jane will agree to pretty much anything on a Sunday morning in exchange for an hour's peace.

"Where's the superglue, Dad?" Tom asked. "I'll need that to stick it back together." My heart sank. The combination of my son and superglue was unthinkable. As a family we've managed to avoid A&E for the last two years. I had no wish to break that record by explaining to Casualty that I'd encouraged my son to glue a Northern Rock mug to his hand.

I sighed, abandoned my ridiculous fantasy of reading the sports section and said, "I'll do it for you." I'm not much good at the DIY end of the father-son spectrum, but gluing? Even I can do that.

Tom went to the cupboard and found the mug. Chipped wasn't an adequate description. Smashing it and gluing it back together was the kindest option. He raced outside to hurl it at the kitchen wall. Then he remembered the idea was to re-arrange the mug, not scatter it to the four corners of the garden. He put his sensible head on and fetched a carrier.

The mug was smashed, half a dozen pieces were rescued and Tom instructed me to start gluing. Thirty minutes later he stood back and surveyed our handiwork – a somewhat open plan mug with jagged sides put on upside down. "It looks a bit like the Sydney Opera House," I said helpfully. No-one else saw the resemblance. Tom pronounced himself satisfied – which translated as "I've had enough now and want to get back to the computer."

"Go on then," I said. "There's one bit left at the bottom – I'll glue it on for you." I smiled to myself – at long last I'd managed to do something creative with my son without it all going horribly wrong. Or so I thought.

"Fetch your mother – quickly," I yelled sixty seconds later.

"Why?" someone shouted back.

"Because I've just superglued myself to this mug, that's why…"

Language Barrier

Just occasionally I'll see a Coke can lying seductively on the ground. After all this time I should know better but I still can't resist kicking it – well, blasting it into the goal actually, leaving the 'keeper clutching thin air. And yes, I do know that I'll look ridiculous tottering into town on my zimmer frame still dribbling a stone along the pavement. What is it about men? When they've reached an age where they should be seriously worrying about pensions, why are they still trying to bend Coke cans like Beckham?

Tom was late at school the other day, so I was traipsing across the playground to collect him. There was a red pot of something lying on the ground, and a rubbish bin providing one excellent goalpost. That crisp packet would do for the other, so naturally I clipped the red thing towards the goal. Absolutely awesome, outside of my right foot, into the bottom left hand corner, in off the bin.

I was so pleased with myself I bent down to see what I'd kicked. "Head Funk," it said on the pot. And underneath, "Extreme Styling Putty." I beg your pardon?

Putty was something my Dad put round the new glass in the window after my football had gone through it. It was grey and stodgy looking. Now people were putting it on their hair?

Could it be me that was mildly out of touch? I'd worked out that it was only 54 weeks until Tom became a teenager – perhaps it was time to learn the language. Forget my thoughts about learning Spanish – teenage suddenly seemed more important.

I already knew some of the basics. Jane hopefully still finds me 'fit', and I've been known to use 'awesome,' (see above, please). Tom has treated me to 'Yeah, right,' which I believe translates as 'I don't believe you, Dad, but I can't be bothered to argue.'

Mercifully 'Whatever' hasn't reared its ugly head in our house – yet. But my favourite – especially when the children are nagging me over something totally pointless, is 'Talk to the hand 'cos the face ain't listening.' Very satisfying.

But hang on, what's monging? And should I worry if my children are mackin'? Three or four conversations with friends who had teenagers – and were prepared to talk about them – produced a spectacular list that I had precisely no idea about. As well as monging and mackin' there were biters, butter, flash, fly, kickin', phat, postal, tight and way.

Jane always claims she's far more in tune with popular culture than me – well, she watches *X-Factor* and *Big Brother* – so I tried the list on her. She didn't have a clue, thank goodness. Tom didn't fare much better, but Jessica astonished me…

"What am I doing if I'm monging around, Jess?"

"Nothing."

"Mackin'?"

"Relaxing, chilling…"

251

Two out of two – clearly the extra hours she devotes to watching TV while Tom's on the computer are paying dividends. Or maybe she simply listens to what's said to her.

"Biters?" She shook her head. "Butter..." No response. "Flash?"

"You just said something really dumb."

But she was totally defeated by 'Phat.' In fact with the exception of one teenager, everyone looked blank – so here's your big chance to be one up when that lump on the settee says, "Pass me the phone book and I'll ring someone who cares." Phat – it means 'fine' or 'cool' – as in Pretty Hot And Tempting.

So bring it on – 54 weeks and counting. I'm ready to be the father of a teenage son – I only hope my wife understands when I tell her she's "Well phat..."

The Beautiful Game

Nathan's Mum takes the coffee, we take the biscuits – and then we stand on the touchline and freeze to death. I have the feeling I should be reading about 'Pools latest win and eating a bacon sandwich, but the water squelching up through my shoes and the wind howling straight from Siberia are telling me otherwise.

First it was Jessica's football taking my Saturday morning away – now Ben's done the same for Sunday. I'm under no illusions about my son – Roman Abramovich will not shortly be knocking on my door – but he's keen and all the matches seem to be at home, so that's me sorted until Easter.

They play 5-a-side at Ben's age. Unfortunately, both teams have twelve players. The coaches put their heads together and decide there'll be two games. Ben's in the second game – I could have had my bacon sandwich after all. To make sure everyone gets a game Phil the coach says there'll be "continuous rolling substitutions" – so it'll be just like watching an England friendly.

Ben's 'A' team run out in orange and black – and so do the other team. Come on, you sponsors – no change strip for the under-7's? What's the world coming to? Eventually, Ben's team are given some red training bibs – putting them on over the orange shirts certainly brightens up the morning. Two or three spectators reach for sunglasses, but whether that's for the colour clash or the after effects of Saturday night I'm not sure.

The standard is surprisingly high. There's even something I've never seen before – six year olds passing to each other. But it's the parents – the ones that still believe they'll be on Jose Mourinho's Christmas card list – that are really worth watching.

"Mark him up, stick with him."

"Come deep, Sean, make some space."

"Man on, Kyle…"

And then there's the inevitable. "Look, he's taking our Robbie off. I can't believe it. I've always known that man was an idiot…"

"Maybe I'm too old," I say to Jane. "I can't believe I'll ever get that worked up. I'll leave it to Phil."

She looks at me sceptically. This is the father who performed a one-man Mexican wave when his son won the frog jumping race on Sports Day.

Eventually Ben and his mates jog on to the pitch. It's not so much a football match as a posse in search of the ball. Ben's team attacks. Nathan shoots and hits the post. The posse charge down to the other end, they shoot – and hit the post as well. Excitement? You could watch England for ten years and not see this much action. We charge back to the other end. Nathan shoots again – amazingly he hits the post again. But this time Ben is running in. The ball cannons back off the post, hits him on the knee and goes in.

Naturally, I go ballistic. It's only Jane hanging on to my arm that stops me running round the pitch with my jumper over my head.

As the game wears on some of the younger ones are – how can I put this – not quite as involved as they should be. "For Pete's sake, Tyler," one mother yells out, "Stop sucking your thumb and get stuck in." There you go, Sven. Midfield not performing at the World Cup? That's what to shout.

Eventually Ben's team win 10-0 and we go home happy. We're just climbing into the car when Phil reminds us that the club is having a fund raising race night in the local scout hut. Astonishingly both Jane and I find we have prior commitments – but there'll be no escape next Sunday...

Memories For Sale

I walked into the lounge last week and found the children watching *Tots TV*. Blimey – I thought we'd waved goodbye to Tilly, Tom and Tiny about four years ago. It was never one of my favourites, and now that Tom's doing French at school I can tell you that all those years of chanting 'sac magique' did him no good whatsoever.

For a couple of days I was worried that all the old videos were going to enjoy a revival. I'm quite happy to sit through a DVD with my children now that it's *Troy* or *King Arthur* – but let's leave *Rosie and Jim* as a mercifully fading memory.

I needn't have worried. Jane took one look at the dining room on Saturday morning and decreed that there was going to be a mass clear out – starting with the videos and the books. My children's formative years will be coming shortly to a car boot sale near you. I was ordered to tackle the books. *Three Little Pigs…Wide-Mouthed Frog…*and look, here's *Thomas the Tank Engine*. I shall miss good old Thomas. I'd sit on the bed with Tom and read one of those little hardbacks nearly every night. I found the one where Thomas was stuck in the snow. Fancy refusing to wear his snow-plough – and driver told him it was going to be deep in the valley. He is a silly engine, isn't he?

(Sorry about that – it's amazing how quickly you regress).

I couldn't wait for Ben to be old enough for Thomas – and he wasn't interested at all. Whatever Ben thought, Thomas wasn't going to the car boot. There was plenty to sell – all those pop-up books that didn't, for a start – but now there would be a box for my grandchildren as well. Thomas might have to spend twenty-five years waiting in the loft, but he could be stuck in the snow one more time.

Not that there was any point in the videos waiting that long. There wouldn't be any machines left to play them on. I counted 81 on the shelves, including *Carol Vorderman's Detox Diet*. Goodness knows where that came from, but you won't be surprised to know I've never watched it.

I put Postman Pat in the sale box and sighed. Another one I'll miss – not so much Pat himself, but I did have a soft spot for Dr Gilbertson. Any time the children knocked themselves I could put on my best Welsh accent and say, "Nothing to worry about, Pat. It's only a sprain."

And the films – *Hercules, Toy Story 2, Mask of Zorro*. Now I came to think of it there were quite a lot that I'd enjoyed. Jane wouldn't notice if the box wasn't completely full, and the video still worked – just.

With a trembling hand I put two more on the 'keep for now' shelf – *Scooby Doo* and *Spy Kids 3D*. I can't come up with an adjective to describe *Scooby Doo*, but it's a masterpiece compared to *Spy Kids 3D*. We first saw it in a deserted cinema in the middle of winter. The children loved it. I wondered what would get me first – insanity, boredom or hypothermia.

And here it was, my all time favourite children's film – *A Knight's Tale*. In my opinion this film includes the most useful phrase a father can learn. Step forward the Black Prince in all his majesty – and what does he say? "This is my solemn word, and as such is beyond contestation."

What more do you need to say to a child? Although it does lose some of the regal splendour when the next four words are, "Now eat your cabbage…"

The Accidental Terrorist

All things considered, the holiday didn't get off to the best start – and inevitably, it was my fault. When we had to cancel our summer holiday the very nice insurance company gave us our money back. Then we discovered that a cottage in Derbyshire in July translates to a villa in Greece at half term. Or it would do, if your seven year old son wasn't arrested as a terrorist.

The day before we flew tempers were a little strained. Having done all the packing, organised the tickets and changed the money, Jane's patience was marginally on the thin side. Rashly, she left me in charge of supervising the children's hand luggage. Naturally I immediately delegated the task.

"Ben, sort your back pack out will you?"

"What shall I put in it?"

"Whatever you like as long as you do it yourself."

In retrospect, that wasn't the wisest thing I've ever said.

Having guided Tom and Jessica through the airport scanner without them triggering an international alert I was ready to reward myself with a full English breakfast – until I heard a commotion behind me. A security man was wearing an 'I've nailed Al-Qaeda' expression. Jane was looking furious and Ben was howling.

"I'm sorry, Madam," I heard him say. "We have to confiscate all potentially lethal weapons."

He was triumphantly waving Ben's plastic gun – another victory in the war on terror. So much for the bacon and eggs – it looked like I'd be posting bail. "Could I ask who let the young man pack this, Madam?" Jane's gaze swung menacingly towards me. I rapidly scanned the departures board. There weren't any planes leaving for the Falklands.

The situation didn't improve when we landed. The villa was in the mountains – which meant that I had to drive…on the wrong side of the road, for the first time in my life, in Greece. The rental lady was all smiles. "Much bigger car," she said, forcing a set of keys on me. "No Golf. Instead, Jumpy."

A Citreon Jumpy…Well, the nine seats would be handy if we adopted some more children. I needed a trusty Golf, not a bus. I'd already been having sleepless nights about hairpin bends with sheer drops – and as I rapidly discovered, the Greeks really know how to encourage terrified drivers. There were little shrines dotted along the roadside. "What are those?" I asked Jane.

"Don't worry," she said. "They're just where someone's died."

But first we needed food – and beer – from the supermarket. This involved my debut left turn in Greek traffic and Jane's simultaneous conversion to the power of prayer. I thought 24 cans would see me through the week. I popped the slab of Amstel on top of the luggage, where it wobbled ominously.

And then we reached the mountains – and a

succession of shrine covered hairpins. "Look at the lovely view, children," Jane trilled, desperately trying to divert them from the driver's bad language. I was so busy avoiding the abyss that I didn't spot a particularly vicious pothole. The beer lurched forward and dealt Tom a savage blow on the right ear. "Well done, dear," Jane said. "That's Ben arrested and Tom with concussion. What have you got in mind for Jessica?"

But I gradually improved and eventually I was trundling down the middle of the road like a Greek version of Postman Pat, waving at everyone I saw. I was quite proud of myself until Jessica turned up. "No offence, Dad, but…" This didn't sound like good news – and she didn't try to be diplomatic. "We still think you're going to drive off a cliff. What's the Greek word for taxi…"

Cronia Polla to you

There you are – too much knowledge can be a dangerous thing. I spent the week before our holiday in Greece poring over long range weather forecasts. The message was simple – rain every day – and I was thoroughly miserable. Friday looked especially bad. The Greek weatherman forecast 'PMT-storms.' At first I thought that was a warning to stay clear of my wife's temper. Then I noticed the adjoining picture of Zeus's lightning bolts and realised it meant thunderstorms in the afternoon.

What had I worried about? Friday came and there we were in the beach restaurant, the sun beating down for the fourth day in a row. The children were building Helms Deep out of sand, there was an empty plate of swordfish in front of me, and Stavros the owner was insisting I have another beer with him. Fly home in three days? No thanks.

I could see Jane looking at me, but it would be rude to refuse the beer. "Your wife," I said, trying to be a new Greek man, "She cook lovely meal. She want a drink?"

Stavros looked at me as though I was insane. "Wife? No drink. She washing up now." There's a woman that needs to spend some time with Jane.

I was totally at peace with the world. Then Jane

said, "So what are we going to do about Tom's birthday?" I'd almost forgotten – Tom was twelve on the last day of the holiday. My plans for tomorrow – sit by the pool, drink Amstel, read four day old English paper – were swiftly jettisoned.

"Why don't I go and find a cake and some candles?" I suggested.

"Because last time you did that you brought back insecticide candles," my wife gently reminded me. Sadly she was right. Jane's birthday had once coincided with another foreign holiday. I'd triumphantly bought the only candles the shop had – it wasn't until the cake was surrounded by dead flies that we realised what I'd done.

"Go and find somewhere," Jane said, "And tell them about Tom's birthday."

So while the family slapped on the factor ten, I scoured Greece in the Citroen Jumpy. I pulled up outside a likely looking taverna. An old woman in traditional black sat on the front step, a 12 bore shotgun resting on her knees. Either migrating sparrows were in season, or you cancelled a booking at your peril.

The lady inside looked much more approachable. Well, she wasn't armed.

"Yassou," I said. "You speak English?"

"A little."

I smiled. "Tomorrow, my son, his birthday."

She beamed back. "Cronia Polla! Happy Birthday."

"You do cake?"

"Chocolada?" No need for a translation there.

"Five people," I said. "Seven o'clock. Twelve years

old." She beamed again. Or seven people, twelve o'clock, five years old. This was Greece – what did it matter?

She told me her name was Dana, and by the time I left we were best friends. It seemed churlish to shake hands, so I gave her a hug. She hugged me back enthusiastically. Hopefully Shotgun Maria wasn't her mother-in-law...

The party was a huge success. Dana even found candles – proper ones. And thanks to Ben she now knows the traditional version of the song: "Cronia Polla to you, stick your head down the loo."

As I lay in bed that night an underground train raced past, directly under the house. At least that's what it felt like. It turned out to be an earthquake, twenty miles away – force six, somebody told us. Not that serious – after all, Tom coming downstairs in a hurry is force four. But suddenly, going home didn't seem like such a bad idea...

Ten More Years

Jane obviously hadn't given me enough jobs to do last weekend because I had time to read an online survey. Apparently parenting is harder than it was a generation ago. We feel guilty, we're not spending enough time with our children, we can't cope without help – and it's become especially difficult over the last ten years.

Well of course it has. Ten years ago Tom was two, Jessica was four months and Ben was an extra bottle of red wine waiting to ambush us one Saturday night. From what I can remember, Tom was teething, but at least he replied every time you spoke to him – and I could use my own computer more than once a week. Jessica was refusing to sleep at night – so nothing's changed there, except that the lullaby machine's gone to the car boot sale.

Be warned – if you've a couple of children around two and you think it's tough now, just you wait. And remember to hide the red wine.

But what about ten years on? Will it be any easier? And what sort of state will I be in? I'm not going to tell you how old I'll be but there was a bloke on our holiday photos with significant signs of grey hair – if there's a makeover programme that needs a challenge, look no further.

Tom will be twenty-two, Jessica twenty and Ben seventeen. Ideally, Tom will have graduated from university, found himself a good job, be saving up for his first house and regularly say, "Thanks, Mum and Dad, I really appreciate all the sacrifices you made for me."

Sadly the evidence from friends with children in their twenties suggests otherwise. Blimey, they're a depressing lot, with their defeated expressions and the lines of worry gouged deep into their faces.

The first thing they always say is, "He's still living at home." Invariably this is followed by a horrifying description of how many pork pies a twenty two year old can eat after a night drinking beer. We might as well order the supersize fridge now. Then they sigh and hit you with the punchline. "And we've had to sort his finances out – again."

Of course I worry about drink and drugs, but not as much as I worry about debt. Jane Austen might have a different slant today. "It is a truth universally acknowledged that a single man not in possession of a good fortune must be in want of a loan and several credit cards – quickly followed by a consolidation loan."

"No," I said to Tom the other day. "We can't afford it and that's final."

"Here you are, Dad," he said, thirty seconds later.

It was the evening paper, neatly folded at the loans page. Right now school are busy teaching him how to tell someone if he's being bullied – all good worthy stuff. I just wish they'd teach him how to turn the TV off when that nice lady from the finance company comes on.

Whatever it takes, I'm going to teach the children how to handle money – and thanks to my friend Sally, I have a plan. She gives her twins an allowance at the beginning of every month, and it covers everything – dinner money, sports, sweets – even the fiver-in-the-birthday-card it currently costs to send my children to a party. If they've spent it all by the 5th, (computer game, Tom?), that's tough. But if they've a surplus at the end of the month, congratulations. So we'll see how it works – and at least when I'm skint by the twentieth I should be able to borrow off Jessica…

A Disgusting Column

A seriously unattractive plant sits proudly on my bedside table, resisting all Jane's attempts to throw it out. Ben was eating a particularly strange piece of fruit one day. I must have been watching *Blue Peter* because I suddenly said, "Come on, finish that and I'll plant the seed for you. We'll grow a fruit tree." Two years later it's a foot tall and has six dark green corrugated leaves. I've no idea what it is but I'm emotionally attached to it and, whatever my wife thinks, I'm determined to keep it alive.

Phone calls from school are never good news are they? They don't ring to say, "Thought you'd like to know, Ben came top in the spelling test. Knew you wouldn't want to wait until teatime to find out." You answer the phone, it's school and the rest of the day is ruined. Ten minutes later you're loading a child into the car, fervently praying that he can make it home without being sick in the back.

Ben – with two equally pale classmates – was sitting in the secretary's office. "It's my Dad," he shouted when he saw me. "I'm going home." I thought I was there under false pretences, but one look at the front of his jumper changed all that.

He fell asleep in the car – so no need to worry about valeting – but his eyes opened as soon we stopped.

"Come on," I said, "Let's get you into a nice, warm bed." Unfortunately that meant our bed. Ben's bed is up a ladder – Jane vetoed the idea of a child vomiting from on high a long time ago.

If you're not feeling too good yourself it may be wise to stop reading now. I put Ben on our bed, he rolled over to the other side and threw up on the carpet – our almost new, largely cream, bedroom carpet. Sitting here calmly I now realise that the waste paper bin was only about three feet away. Why didn't I think that at the time? Instead I tried to catch it in my hands. I stood there pathetically with the school's idea of mixed vegetables dripping steadily onto the carpet.

Oh no, it was coming again. I looked round in panic and grabbed the nearest thing I could. My plant. Ben vomited on it spectacularly.

Eventually he stopped. Somehow I got him changed and into bed. Then I surveyed the damage. The idea of telling Jane that the carpet had a few extra orange flecks was not attractive. What should I do about the stain – not to mention the smell? For some reason my Dad knew the solution to every household disaster – rinse it in soda water, dab it with vinegar, iron it with blotting paper. Another gene I hadn't inherited...

With a flash of inspiration I dashed downstairs and typed "remove vomit stains" into Google. I had visions of Jane coming home to find me rubbing tomato sauce into the carpet. "It's a traditional remedy, darling," I'd say condescendingly. "Didn't your Mother teach you anything?"

For once, Google failed me. All it suggested was

spending a large amount of money on American carpet cleaner. Maybe warm water was the answer.

That was how Jane found me when she came home – on my knees, dabbing away. "Looks like you might be finished in an hour," she said and went off to make a cup of tea.

She popped her head back round the door. "Was he sick anywhere else?"

"On my plant, if you must know."

"Really?" she said, completely failing to suppress a smile. "I hope he hasn't killed it, dear…"

Mud & Mystery

Tom came home from school last Friday with a map of Australia on his trousers – Brisbane was nicely centred on his left buttock. There was a cow on his knee and the Milky Way down the length of one leg – all in mud, of course. Yes, we're grateful the school still has a playing field – I just wish my son wouldn't come home wearing it.

How does he manage to get so dirty when all he'll admit to doing at break-time is talking about *Little Britain?* Like many things in my pre-teenage son's life, it's a complete mystery to me.

Explain this. He is clinically incapable of putting anything away. Clothes, food, computer games – nothing is returned to its rightful home. Except when it's empty. Once or twice a week I'm amazed to find the packet of Crunchy Nut Cornflakes back where it should be – and then I find two lonely flakes marooned at the bottom of the bag. It's the same with the milk. Bottle half full? Leave it on the worktop, preferably next to the little pool that didn't make it to the bowl. But an empty bottle? Good as gold, Tom puts that back in the fridge.

But back to dirt – specifically, his shirts. What's going on in year seven? I remember the advert on TV. Every stain known to man, waiting for the miracle washing powder to dissolve them. "Stupid," I thought, "No-one can get grass, mud, ink, gravy, paint and lipstick all on one shirt." A twelve year old boy can – well, five out of six. And once Tom discovers what happens behind the bike sheds he'll have the full set.

Life's settled into a simple pattern. Tom comes home from school: we attack his uniform with the clothes brush. Or we did until the weekend, when the clothes brush simply disappeared. Somewhere in our house there's a tear in the space/time fabric – it's the only explanation for the keys, TV remotes, shoes and now clothes brush that vanish without trace. I was sent out into the cold to buy a new one. "And buy a good stiff one," Jane ordered.

I started my search at the hardware shop on the corner. The owner is close to being my best friend. Whenever I can't fix something he explains what I have to do and sells me the exact number I need, even if it's one and it costs 10p. Tom had a science project last year: two minutes of advice, a piece of wire and a light bulb and my son had a gold star.

"What's broken now?" my friend asked when I walked in.

"My wife's patience. Where do you keep the clothes brushes?" I was confident I'd soon be home.

For the first time ever he shook his head. "Try the dry cleaners," he suggested, seeing my look of despair. Hartlepool was now significantly colder than the Antarctic. I trudged up the road with all the enthusiasm of Captain Oates.

No joy. "Sorry, dear. Why don't you try a dog brush? Pet shop round the corner..."

I didn't fancy another freezing walk, but the idea of brushing Tom down like a muddy springer spaniel did have a certain appeal.

"What sort of dog is it?"

"It isn't," I said. "It's a twelve year old boy." Mrs. Pet Shop didn't bat an eyelid – clearly I wasn't the first. For £2.99 she presented me with a splendidly lethal weapon – stiff bristles on one side, wire spikes on the other. And it made mincemeat of the map of Australia. I'm going back next week to see what she recommends for empty cornflake packets...

Macho Man

How can I possibly have another cold? I religiously drink orange juice every morning (no, not the stuff with real oranges in it – that's far too expensive), I eat enough garlic to keep a flock of vampires at bay and yet here I am. For the second time in two months I'm surrounded by nasal sprays and tissues, with my nose running like a river in flood. Meanwhile my children carry on as normal, resolutely avoiding my germs and refusing to come within three feet of me.

Tom is particularly irritating. I make a determined effort to meet the Government's "five a day" target. People have received New Year's Honours for less. My eldest son, meanwhile, lives on cornflakes and peanut butter and wouldn't recognize a vegetable if he woke up in bed with one. But when did he last have a cold? Not this year, not last year – in fact I can't ever remember the wretched boy going round with a box of tissues under his arm.

Maybe he's simply tougher than I am. Maybe I should stop nagging him about fresh air and exercise and start eating more cornflakes.

What makes it even worse is that he never wears a coat, however cold it is. I'd wear three if it wasn't for the fact that even one makes me look like a Michelin man.

"Tom, it's freezing outside, you need your coat on this morning."

"No, I don't, it's not that cold."

"Tom, I have spent the last five minutes scraping the car windscreen. Now will you please put a coat on?"

"I don't need one."

"Why not?"

"Because nobody wears a coat to school."

And they don't. Like everyone else in his class, Tom simply refuses to wear his coat.

Who cares if the temperature in Hartlepool is equivalent to liquid nitrogen? Year seven are a macho bunch and their parents aren't going to change them. I distinctly remember wearing a variety of anoraks when I was at secondary school – I'm sure one of them was purple. Then I spent one year in a duffle coat, looking like a cross between Adrian Mole and a peace protester. No wonder the girls found me so easy to resist.

But the real pinnacle of my sartorial elegance was at junior school – my balaclava. It was about a mile from our house to school, and as soon as the first frosts appeared, on went the balaclava Mum had knitted. The pain involved in that balaclava. "Stand up straight," she'd order me. "Put your arms out in front of you. Now where's the navy blue…" And after half an hour's torture she'd finally finish winding the wool into a ball.

What's the possibility of that happening now? Jane deciding to sit down and knit a balaclava, Ben being prepared to wear one and – most unlikely of all –

Tom removing his arms from the computer to allow her to wind the wool. My calculator won't go that high.

When I was seven I used to think you could look pretty cool in a balaclava – push it back off your head, so it was just round your neck and pretend you were Richard the Lionheart. Well, I thought I looked cool.

I could probably sell the idea to Ben. "OK, Ben, put this over your head and then push it back like that and you'll look like you're in *Kingdom of Heaven*..."

Ben likes knights – he might go for it. Until Jessica offered her opinion. My daughter's judgements on other people's clothes make Trinny and Susannah seem like supportive angels. Ben in a balaclava? Jessica would emotionally scar him for life...

The Empty Box Shop

Come on – there are only twelve phoning days left until Christmas. Still, I should look on the bright side – there were about thirty when Tom started his onslaught. He's been seduced by the new Xbox 360. He's offered me all his birthday money and found a buyer for the old one, so he's skillfully managed to bring it within the budget for his Christmas present. The trouble is, unless you ordered one around 1998 your chances of a pre-Xmas delivery are significantly below zero. My son will not accept this.

He now dogs my footsteps with a list of every retailer within a thirty mile radius and the words "But Nathan got one…" So Nathan did, by virtue of his mother driving a hundred miles, queuing for several days and spending four times what I spent on my first car. "OK," I finally said, "Pass me the phone. Ten minutes – and then let me watch the football."

I tried a large national retailer and listened patiently to seven pre-recorded options. None of them applied. Option eight told me to contact my local store. Thanks for that. I looked up the number – there wasn't one. All they offered was the number I'd just rung. Option one might as well say, "Don't waste your time listening to this. Waste it in a traffic jam trying to reach the shop instead."

Tom therefore decided that a Sunday morning trip to town was required. Jane and Jessica would drop him off and give him a couple of hours to harass every possible retailer. Jessica, meanwhile, had nagged her Mother into some serious retail therapy.

"So Tom," I said as he left, "What do you do if a complete stranger comes up to you, says he knows a shop where they have Xbox 360's in stock and why don't you go with him?"

Tom looked wistfully into space. "Is there a shop like that?" Good to know the school's awareness lessons are working.

I was enjoying the peace and quiet at home when the phone rang. "I've found a shop, Dad," Tom yelled excitedly. "They've definitely got them in stock."

"How do you know?"

"There are boxes of them on the shelves. Can you phone Mum? Ask her to meet me. Quick, before they sell out…"

I rang Jane and persuaded her to rush down the road and meet Tom. Jessica would be heavily into her shopping. I was glad it wasn't me dragging her off to go and look at a games console.

Jane phoned me back fifteen minutes later. She didn't sound pleased. "The boxes were empty."

"What do you mean the boxes were empty?"

"Tom didn't bother to ask in the shop. They were for display…" The phone was snatched off my wife. I distinctly heard my daughter saying, "Let me talk to him."

"Daddy?" Even Mrs. Thatcher had never been this angry. Tom was about to learn a valuable lesson. "I was just trying some new clothes on. And I had to come out of the changing room…" If my son had any sense he'd keep a very low profile for the next six months. "…To go and look at an empty box."

If – like me – you've been married for around 140 years you'll know that a wife never forgets anything, especially if you've embarrassed her, missed a significant date or said the wrong thing. I strongly suspect a sister might be exactly the same. Thirty years from now they'll be at some family do and Ms Sarcastic will say, "That's right, Tom. Just like the time you made us all go to a shop that sold empty boxes…"

Hollywood Calling

The news came through three weeks ago. At first it was only a rumour on the school grapevine. Then it was down to the final two. The envelope eventually arrived. We opened it with trembling hands.

And the winner is... Yes! At long last we'd done it. After eight or nine years of trying – am I really that old? – our family had finally landed the lead role in the school nativity play. "Ben has been chosen to play the part of the grumpy innkeeper." Magnificent casting, Mrs. Reed. Ben is to star in her rib-tickling, infant production of – trumpets, fanfare, you guessed it – *The Grumpy Innkeeper.*

Once upon a time Jessica was Mary in the very same play. "But we are very tired," she wailed, knocking pitifully on the inn door, "We have travelled through night and day."

Adam Bright wrenched the door open. "Hard luck," he roared, "That's not my problem. I'm off to bed..." And with that he stormed upstairs, leaving Mary and Joseph shivering on the doorstep. What a part – if Johnny Depp had seen the script he wouldn't have given *Pirates of the Caribbean* a second glance.

As soon as the letter arrived we went into feverish rehearsals – 'feverish' being the right word, thanks to my never-ending cold. Having played the innkeeper to Jessica's Mary, now it was my turn to be Mary – and Joseph – and the shepherds – and the wise men. Grumpy gives them all the same answer. "Clear off! In the stable! Round the back!"

And Mrs. Innkeeper… "Would you like one of your pills, dear?" I asked ('very nervously', according to Mrs. R's stage directions).

"No, I would not," Ben yelled. I tell you, he was brilliant – so brilliant that I forgot myself, and, full of cold, gave him an enormous hug and kiss. Whoops…

You know that moment when a child suddenly goes droopy? And you realise that all you'll be doing in the wee, small hours is doling out the Calpol. It happened at 6:00pm on Sunday. No bath, no hair-wash, just straight to bed with a bumper bottle of the pink stuff. The Government is thinking about parenting classes? "A large bottle of Calpol please, and one for next month while I'm here." There, job done.

Monday morning came. Ben had a temperature and an ominously persistent cough. No matter – it was dress rehearsal day. Whatever his state of health, he was going to school. The idea of having to tell Mrs. Reed that the star of the show was in bed was unthinkable. "The show must go on," I told him – with no confidence that it would.

It was my day to collect the children. "How did it go?" I asked Ben. "Fine," he muttered, his voice barely audible. He climbed into the back of the car and fell asleep. He woke up at home long enough to have a coughing fit and two slugs of Calpol. And that was Monday.

He was no better the next morning, but Tuesday was crucial – the performance for the rest of the school, with the Butcher of Broadway (his sister, who else?) in the front row. Four o'clock came – he croaked "fine" at Jane and once more crashed out in the car.

Back at home the arch-critic delivered her judgement. "He was..." she paused dramatically, "...Not bad." High praise indeed.

The big day arrived – Wednesday, Showtime. "Break a leg, treasure," I told him.

"Isn't a cold good enough, Dad?" he coughed back.

How did he do? A lot better than "not bad." I bought three of the school's DVD's. One for us, one for Grandma – and one for Johnny Depp's agent...

We Three Boys

"Are you sure about that?" Josh's Mum asked, looking at me extremely doubtfully. George's father simply couldn't believe it. He shook his head slowly, told me he knew where counselling was available and promised to have the hot chocolate waiting.

Every year – in true festive spirit – I force my children to go carol singing. Or I did until this year. Tom claimed an urgent appointment with the Xbox, and Jessica refused to desert Colin Jackson on *Strictly Come Dancing*. Or maybe they've just become too cool to be seen carol singing with their Dad.

Fortunately Ben came to my rescue. Given that three was the traditional number, two of his friends – George and Josh – were invited, much to the bewilderment of their respective parents, both of whom were settling down with red wine and the remote control.

The boys were impatient to begin, so I parked the car on the nearest development of not-quite-executive houses. If the number of flashing Santas sliding down the roofs was any guide, there was plenty of disposable income.

Having been very much the junior partner for the last few years, Ben was now determined to be Boss. "We'll start off with *Away in a Manger*," he declared,

"And it's George's job to say 'A very Merry Christmas'. He's the youngest and cutest."

I almost wiped away a tear – what a lovely thought.

"It's true," Ben went on. "Everyone will love George, so they'll give us more money – and if they give us a lot, we'll say 'Happy New Year' as well."

It didn't quite go according to plan at the first house. Josh rang the bell and... nothing happened. Before I could shout "Don't do that," George was looking through the lounge window.

"They're hiding behind the sofa," he said.

I ask you. What is the point of pretending to be in the Christmas spirit by decorating your front garden with a glow-in-the-dark nativity scene if you then cower behind your furniture to avoid three small boys?

Thirty minutes later we arrived at The House. That's all you say where we live. "Have you been to see The House yet?" It has raised Christmas bling to a new level, and become a serious tourist attraction. "Look at you three," said Mrs. Bling when she answered the door, "How cute are you?" I could feel them blushing from the bottom of the drive. She was so busy telling the boys how cute they were that she didn't spot her extremely large dog escaping. Fortunately he only wanted to relieve himself on an inflatable purple reindeer.

"One more house," I finally said to the boys, "And then it's hot chocolate time." A sprightly old lady came to the door. She was treated to a particularly fine version of *Rudolph* and joined in lustily towards the end.

"That's beautiful," she said. "What charity are you collecting for?"

Ben looked at me, seriously puzzled. Charity? Chocolate if he had his way. "Er... the Hospice," I suddenly heard myself say.

"Oh, yes," she beamed. "How suitable." And she handed Ben a £5 note. It took me about twenty minutes to stop him saying "Happy Christmas."

Needless to say there was no way I could prise the fiver off the boys – so I ended the evening frozen stiff and in debt to the Hospice.

Late that night I crept into Ben's room to turn off his light. Suddenly he sat bolt upright in bed. "Merry Christmas," he shouted in his sleep. "And a Happy New Year. Thank you very much." I couldn't have put it better myself...